THE NEW WORK OF WRITING ACROSS THE CURRICULUM

THE NEW WORK OF WRITING ACROSS THE CURRICULUM

Diversity and Inclusion, Collaborative Partnerships, and Faculty Development

STACI M. PERRYMAN-CLARK

UTAH STATE UNIVERSITY PRESS
Logan

© 2023 by University Press of Colorado

Published by Utah State University Press
An imprint of University Press of Colorado
1580 North Logan Street, Suite 660
PMB 39883
Denver, Colorado 80203-1942

 The University Press of Colorado is a proud member of the Association of University Presses.

The University Press of Colorado is a cooperative publishing enterprise supported, in part, by Adams State University, Colorado State University, Fort Lewis College, Metropolitan State University of Denver, University of Alaska Fairbanks, University of Colorado, University of Denver, University of Northern Colorado, University of Wyoming, Utah State University, and Western Colorado University.

∞ This paper meets the requirements of the ANSI/NISO Z39.48-1992 (Permanence of Paper).

ISBN: 978-1-64642-452-8 (hardcover)
ISBN: 978-1-64642-453-5 (paperback)
ISBN: 978-1-64642-454-2 (ebook)
https://doi.org/10.7330/9781646424542

Library of Congress Cataloging-in-Publication Data

Names: Perryman-Clark, Staci M., author.
Title: The new work of writing across the curriculum : diversity and inclusion, collabora-tive partnerships, and faculty development / Staci M. Perryman-Clark.
Description: Logan : Utah State University Press, [2023] | Includes bibliographical refer-ences and index.
Identifiers: LCCN 2023014959 (print) | LCCN 2023014960 (ebook) | ISBN 9781646424528 (hardcover) | ISBN 9781646424535 (paperback) | ISBN 9781646424542 (ebook)
Subjects: LCSH: English language—Rhetoric—Study and teaching (Higher)—Social aspects—United States. | Curriculum change—United States. | Anti-racism—Study and teaching (Higher)—United States.
Classification: LCC PE1405.U6 P45 2023 (print) | LCC PE1405.U6 (ebook) | DDC 808/.0420711—dc23/eng/20230515
LC record available at https://lccn.loc.gov/2023014959
LC ebook record available at https://lccn.loc.gov/2023014960

Cover illustration © flovie/Shutterstock.

In loving memory of Freddie Mae Jamison (August 18, 1938–June 7, 2022), who was a collector of all of my scholarly books. May you rejoice with the ancestors as I add another work to your heavenly collection.

CONTENTS

CONTENTS

ACKNOWLEDGMENTS

First and foremost, I wish to thank my Heavenly Father for showing up at the eleventh hour to provide me with the insight needed to complete this book when I was so close to abandoning the project. I would also like to thank my husband, Randall D. Clark, and daughter, Jamison Inez Perryman-Clark, for their sacrifices as I worked long hours to complete this manuscript post-COVID during 2020. I would also like to thank my parents, Reverend Dr. Donald L. Perryman and Willetta Perryman, for being my biggest cheerleaders as I navigated multiple—and at times competing—book projects. Their words of encouragement provided me with the persistence to move forward. And to my big sister and biggest fan, Dr. Tracee L. Perryman, I cannot thank you enough for the long FaceTime conversations and leadership advice you've provided while writing this book. I would also like to thank several of my sisters from another mother, including Sherine Obare, Evelyn Winfield-Thomas, Candy McCorkle, Mariam Konaté, Jennifer Richardson, and Monique Haley, for their guidance, love, and support and for giving me my flowers while I am still here! And to my English Department colleagues, John Saillant, Lisa Cohen Minnick, and Jonathan Bush, thank you for recognizing the value of my work when other institutional colleagues from high and low refused to. In addition, I would like to thank Rachael Levay, my amazing acquisitions editor, who helped me navigate many starts and stops as I began writing this book roughly five years ago! Finally, I would like to thank Jan Gabel-Goes, former director of the WMU Office of Faculty Development, for giving me the canvas needed to create OFD programming. Her faith gave me the freedom to build, develop, and dream, a freedom that I have taken into every administrative and leadership role I've had in faculty development since.

THE NEW WORK OF WRITING
ACROSS THE CURRICULUM

Introduction

COMMITTING TO THE NEW WORK OF WRITING ACROSS THE CURRICULUM
Diversity and Inclusion and Faculty Development

I directed the first-year writing program at Western Michigan University for eight very long years, and I started in 2010, fresh out of a doctoral program and into my first tenure-track position. Over those eight years, I've watched many cohorts of new master's and doctoral students develop from novice and newly minted college writing instructors to confident and dedicated professionals and experts in the teaching of college writing. I've watched these instructors go on to esteemed doctoral programs and tenure-track positions. I've watched them publish pedagogical articles developed from assignments they produced in my courses on teaching writing at the college level. It was a very rewarding experience, and as a scholar I continue to take passion in sharing best practices in the teaching of college writing with colleagues in my field of rhetoric and composition. That said, I began to get bored with directing a first-year writing program year after year.

My schedule of teaching the same college writing prep class for new TAs never changed. Roughly six years into the gig, I felt I was going through the motions. Every summer would include a two-week orientation, with speaker after speaker and session after session. Every fall I would observe new instructors and prepare an observation report for each of them, every spring I would help develop instructional workshops, and at the end of every academic year I would schedule and staff 122 sections with sixty different TAs and part-time instructors. This would repeat year after year after year. After six years in, I knew I needed a change, but I also knew that I still had a passion for providing pedagogical training for how to teach college-level writing. I also knew that this sort of training did not have to happen only in a first-year writing program. It was around this same time period that a position opening for an associate director emerged at Western Michigan University's Office of Faculty Development, or OFD, our institution's teaching and learning center. This was the sort of opportunity I needed. As such, I

https://doi.org/10.7330/9781646424542.c000

wanted to leverage my pedagogical training to show those not trained in English studies how to teach writing in their disciplines. It was in this space, OFD, that I began to work as the associate director to create a writing across the curriculum program. It was also in this space that I first began to reflect on the fact that the work of writing never ends. As long as we work in institutions of higher education, we will be called upon to do the work of writing. And even beyond higher education, we will be called upon to write. Writing and the professionalization of writing instruction continues, and its reach is far beyond first-year writing.

In 2016, I applied for the position of Associate Director of OFD, primarily because WMU lacked a formal writing across the curriculum (WAC) program. Seeking to develop a stronger WAC presence, I determined that from an institutional sense, the only designated location for teaching and learning professional development was OFD. Previously on campus, there had been on-again, off-again efforts by a few writing studies faculty and the campus writing center staff to start a few writing projects, one of which included a self-study of the different writing programs at WMU. The self-study included the First-Year Writing Program I directed, the required first-year writing course for the College of Engineering and Applied Sciences (a first-year technical communication course), the first-year writing required course for WMU's Haworth College of Business (informational writing), and select faculty teaching the courses certified for the University's baccalaureate writing requirement (a third- or fourth-year course focused on writing in students' majors). While the self-study began with some enthusiasm, it was never completed. Other reports simply focused on whether or not graduate students needed their own writing center. During these transitions, the Haworth College of Business shut down its first-year writing course and required their students to enroll in the First-Year Writing Program, housed by the Department of English, where I was director. It then shifted its instructors to a newly formed business and communication center for business students, where students could receive feedback on both oral presentations and writing assignments, therefore duplicating some of the efforts of the campus writing center.

The duplication of resources sought to deal with a bigger problem: the lack of an institutional site to support faculty teaching writing. Faculty would often seek professional development from the writing center and business communication center staff to help them prepare to teach writing; however, these centers were underresourced, and its staff were not formally trained to do professional development for faculty wanting WAC teaching and learning resources. While well-intentioned, these workshops often resorted to classroom visits with faculty and students, with staff describing their services and what students could expect from an appointment with staff. While necessary, these workshops were not fulfilling the needs of faculty: faculty wanted pedagogical professional development that would help them improve their teaching of writing. In effect, they needed the resources that a WAC program might offer. Thus, I was hired as the Associate Director of OFD to create this type of program.

As a scholar whose pedagogical interests also included culturally relevant pedagogies, I also wanted to develop WAC workshops on linguistic diversity and anti-racist teaching practices, something I would do during my tenure at the OFD. However, immediately upon my arrival, I experienced an abundance of women faculty of color needing support and advice for navigating many of the microaggressions associated with the workplace and their academic departments. Many of them needed mentorship and support with navigating the tenure and promotion process, while others were so disenchanted they were seeking ways to leave the institution. Though I had initially come to develop a WAC presence, I found myself spending the bulk of my time working with women of color, serving as advocates as they filed grievances, and reviewing materials in response to adverse decisions about their tenure and promotion cases. I also found faculty reaching out to me for advice on how to address students' complaints regarding faculty microaggressions. I even had students reaching out for advice and support with navigating biases from faculty in the classroom, although our teaching and learning center was designed to serve instructors and not students. As a result, I knew that OFD needed to develop more formal diversity and inclusion programming in conjunction with WAC programming.

Although I am no longer with OFD, the office continues to expand and develop a variety of programming. From all of my current and past administrative roles on campus, OFD was one of the most welcoming, inclusive, and collaborative environments in which I had worked, one that significantly contrasted the work environments I discussed in previously published scholarship (Craig and Perryman-Clark 2016; Perryman-Clark 2016; Perryman-Clark and Craig 2019). It was my refuge, and I was hesitant to leave and also halt any progress WMU would see around WAC and diversity and inclusion outreach. Nonetheless, after being honest with myself, I knew in my heart that I really had aspired to pursue a career in administration, and my institution had only committed to reassigning faculty time for the position, not a full-time senior officer position as I desired. Regardless of the timing of my previous initiatives, I knew I had to pursue a new opportunity.

It wasn't until I began working in additional administrative roles, one as the former associate dean of an honors college and the other as chair of an interdisciplinary institute, that I'd come to recognize how much diversity and inclusion work was tied to WAC outreach and professional development. After meeting with various groups of underrepresented scholars on campus, I initially asked why members from these groups were not joining the honors college despite the college's efforts to recruit a diverse group of students. One director responded that because she knew I had a background in writing, and because I shared a similar racialized subject position to those of the students with whom she works, she would share that her students feared writing the most: in short, they were afraid of writing the honors thesis, the final requirement for graduating from the honors college. They had been told all too frequently by faculty that although they had the required GPA to remain in academic standing in the honors college, they could not write.

When I became a department chair of a unit not within the Department of English, I would soon find out how deep the wounds of racial microaggressions, hostile work environments, and additional traumas felt, especially for BIPOC women in higher education, traumas I've since written about with these colleagues (Perryman-Clark, Konaté, and Richardson 2022). For this reason, I'd later accept an opportunity to serve as the chair and director of the Institute for Intercultural and Anthropological Studies (IIAS), a unit that would house multiple Black women after their exodus from the toxic Gender and Women's Studies department, where I formally held a joint appointment. From this exodus, every BIPOC woman left the department, and three of us moved to IIAS. While my previous scholarship had always argued from the standpoint that diversity work is writing work, particularly as this work relates to writing program administrative (WPA) work, and that honoring lived experiences with racial microaggressions is indeed rhetorical work, it was clear that there needed to be a book written from the standpoint that diversity work is WAC work and WAC work is institutional work. There needed to be a book that made connections between diversity, WAC, and institutional teaching and learning centers. My career trajectory from WPA to faculty developer to academic administrator suggested that it was I who should write this book.

Using my previous positions as Associate Director of Office of Faculty Development (OFD), Director of First-Year Writing, and current position as Chair and Director of IIAS, this book provides a descriptive analysis of how institutions can work collaboratively to foster stronger intellectual activities around writing as connected to campus-wide diversity and inclusion initiatives. It moreover contends that teaching and learning centers and WAC programs gain tremendously from each other by building explicit partnerships on campus-wide diversity initiatives that emphasize cultural competence. In addition, it shows how both cultural competence and written proficiency enhance the transferable skills necessary for completing undergraduate education requirements and how the work of WAC programs and faculty development centers can be leveraged to draw the attention of senior administrative leadership.

This book also provides readers with a practical example of a career trajectory in which writing specialists move from WPA work, to campus-wide work in faculty development centers, and then to administrative positions. From this trajectory, readers see how a background in writing studies provides sets of transferable skills to develop key initiatives and programs in senior-level administration. It moreover reveals the connections between retention and writing programs, and between diversity and inclusion and writing pedagogy. In doing so, it shows how WPAs can continue doing writing as intellectual work beyond writing programs. It further shows how a background in writing studies enhances one's ability to lead and develop college-wide initiatives. Finally, it provides us with the opportunity to be campus-wide champions and leaders for diversity and inclusion.

By making these arguments, this book surveys scholarship that addresses diversity, faculty development, and WAC and finds that many of these initiatives are created in isolation, therefore reinforcing institutional silos; activities that occur in silos often are not leveraged strategically to gain the attention of senior administrators, particularly those working at state-supported public institutions who must manage shrinking institutional budgets due to reductions in state allocations to higher education. In many cases doing this intellectual work in isolation makes stand-alone programs like WAC vulnerable to budget cuts, because senior administrators either do not see this work as campus-wide work or because they see it as a duplication of services done in other units. As such, I argue that such partnerships must be bridged more formally when universities commit and invest in establishing stronger commitments to diversity and inclusion, as many institutions include both written proficiency and diversity and inclusion student learning outcomes. I revisit conversations from Susan McLeod and Margot Soven's collection, *Writing Across the Curriculum: A Guide to Developing Programs*, while also considering Linda Adler-Kassner and Elizabeth Wardle's collection, *Naming What We Know: Threshold Concepts in Writing Studies*, to establish a foundation for the impact of WAC programs on college campuses.

Additional sources, including *Faculty Development in the Age of Evidence*, are also referenced. In short, both writing on WAC and faculty develop-ment literature are positioned in relation to each other to identify the parallels that run across both sets of intellectual work, particularly in response to the ever-increasing needs of working with students from diverse populations.

To provide updates for the importance of providing diversity and inclusion–related professional development in a twenty-first-century context, I argue that both faculty development and WAC need to make diversity and inclusion initiatives a priority for professional develop-ment, as both enhance student learning. Furthermore, these alliances can be strengthened by collaborating formally on diversity and inclu-sion programming. To establish the need for diversity and inclusion programming in both areas, I review both faculty development and WAC initiatives that point to increased understandings of diversity and inclu-sion (Anson 2012; Beach 2016; Cox 2014; Nielsen 2014), with linguistic diversity being one example of programming that WAC specialists might offer with faculty development centers. In essence, this book responds to my call, previously identified in chapter 6 of *Afrocentric Teacher-Research: Rethinking Appropriateness and Inclusion,* for rhetoric and composition to create additional opportunities beyond writing programs to promote linguistic diversity in WAC outreach. The book concludes by offering descriptive analysis and reflection on institutional examples of the ways in which WAC initiatives and faculty development have collaborated formally at Western Michigan University, despite lacking a formal WAC program. These examples of formal collaborations include general edu-cation reform and diversity and inclusion programming. At the founda-tion of these initiatives is the work of faculty development and teaching and learning centers as hubs for making such initiatives possible, par-ticularly in the absence of formal WAC programs.

This introduction, then, orients readers to the processes that inform how my shifts from WPA to faculty developer to academic administra-tor have allowed me to fulfill my passion for diversity and inclusion intellectual work. For me, a shift from WPA work was necessary to develop sustainable diversity and inclusion programming beyond the first-year writing experience. While the shift from WPA in an academic department to a campus-wide leadership role is a natural evolution for WPAs, I argue not only that this shift was critical to my own personal development for improving postsecondary writing instruction across campus, but also that such a shift is necessary for WPAs to consider when committing to doing diversity and inclusion work; this shift has been helpful for navigating senior leadership positions. Such work is necessary to effect larger-scale institutional change, a skill needed in senior-level administration; moreover, stronger collaborations between WAC initiatives and centers for faculty development and teaching and learning are vital steps toward moving diversity and inclusion efforts forward as they pertain to teaching and learning at institutions of higher education.

BRIDGING PARTNERSHIPS: WHY WAC, WHY FACULTY DEVELOPMENT, WHY DIVERSITY, WHY NOW?

It is also important to define precisely what I mean by diversity. Drawing from Mathew Ouellett's (2004) definition of diversity as it relates to faculty development programming, I define diversity to "include a systemic analysis of how such forces work together to hold systems of discrimination and oppression in place" (188). While WAC development and diversity and inclusion programming were two initiatives as part of my OFD portfolio, therefore institutionally and practically connecting the work that I do on both fronts, WPA work and culturally relevant pedagogy have always shaped the work that I do as a scholar; perhaps it is without accident that my portfolio of work at OFD would include both WAC and diversity and inclusion professional development. For the past several years, Collin Craig and I have been calling attention to the challenges associated with confronting microaggressions in WPA work (Craig and Perryman-Clark 2011, 2016; Perryman-Clark and Craig 2019), and I've also (2016) discussed the challenges and microaggressions associated with WPAs charged with doing writing assessment, when the faculty member is a woman of color. As such, professional development and training in implicit bias are closely linked to the professional development that WPAs possess the opportunity to facilitate when assisting faculty with pedagogical strategies for teaching writing more effectively. In other words, inclusive teaching *is* WAC outreach, and teaching and learning centers, like OFD, have been useful platforms for WPAs to become a leading presence for writing instruction and culturally relevant pedagogy on college campuses.

While diversity and inclusion programming has not historically been the primary mission of WAC outreach and program development, this book argues that perhaps it should be, though WAC programs need not bear this responsibility alone. With the help and support of teaching and learning centers, WAC programs can form stronger partnerships with teaching and learning centers to move forward diversity and inclusion initiatives for both faculty and students. To do so, however, WAC and faculty development centers must foster stronger collaborations and partnerships, as opposed to duplicating similar efforts in silos. Thus, faculty development and WAC work are essential for helping universities and divisions fulfill their missions of fostering diversity and inclusion, with equity and justice being the goal.

My rationale for bridging both diversity and inclusion with WAC and faculty development centers also centers around my assumption that both audiences have a tremendous amount to gain from one another. In the absence of formal WAC programs, teaching and learning centers can benefit from the expertise of rhetoric and composition scholars and WPAs. Likewise, writing specialists benefit from more explicit training on inclusive excellence in teaching and on how to overcome implicit biases and microaggressions as educators and writing program administrators. For me, my work has focused on biases associated with race and gender when doing WPA work. In chapter 1 of our collection, *Black Perspectives in Writing Program Administration: From the Margins to the Center* (2019), Collin and I assert: "Centering WPA discourse as intersectional critical race work is an opportunity for exploring these subjects of inquiry as critical interventions. It positions us to cultivate antiracist responses from the perspective of those of color . . . and enact socially responsible approaches to program building" (11).

This is not to suggest that diversity-related topics, especially as they pertain to anti-racist practices, have not been addressed in rhetoric and composition or WPA scholarship. That said, scholars continue to call for the allyship of white WPAs in supporting students and WPAs of color. Scott Wible (2019) contends that "white allies operate with self-awareness about this privilege and are motivated to put this unearned privilege on the line when they have an opportunity to support and advocate for a person of color—and they don't 'just go away when difficulty appears'" (82). Wible further describes his own experiences leading professional development workshops in the teaching of writing, noting:

> During my first seven years as WPA of our professional development program, which delivers the upper-division general education writing course at our university, I tried to make language diversity an area of focus in our professional development and our pedagogy. I led full-day professional development sessions on topics such as helping students build on non-standardized varieties of English and working with multilingual writers, and on three other occasions we hosted nationally recognized composition scholars to facilitate professional development sessions on linguistic diversity in composition classrooms . . . One critical piece missing from these activities, however, is integrating these values toward language

> diversity into mission and vision statements that articulate a social justice mission for our program's teaching and research. (92)

Such an earnest and candid reflection on the implications associated with the ways that writing and WAC specialists can contribute to larger conversations about anti-racist practices. As one notices from Wible's exchange, his professional development workshop is conducted for and with writing faculty; however, Wible's reflection significantly underscores the need for these conversations about writing conventions to be had with faculty who are not writing specialists but teach writing. In effect, Wible's professional development work is potentially also WAC professional development, work that could significantly benefit from collaborations with teaching and learning centers that are structured to reach large populations of faculty.

In addition to anti-racist teaching practices, collaborations with teaching and learning centers enable us to provide richer and more extensive conversations about diversity and inclusive teaching beyond race. However, as I discuss in chapter 5 of this book, collaborations with teaching and learning centers have provided opportunities to work with disability support offices to design accessible teaching materials, as well as opportunities to work with LGBTQ+ offices, faculty, and organizations on campus to design trans-friendly syllabi and curricular materials that affirm students' preferred names and pronouns, for example. Collaborative work with LGBTQ+ constituents has enabled WMU to begin changing restroom facility signs on campus to reflect gender-neutral bathrooms. This work not only benefits the whole institution but also those teaching in writing programs. In essence, WPAs and WAC directors can also benefit from these professional development opportunities offered by centers for faculty development and teaching and learning who possess the institutional space to house and facilitate such collaboration.

SYNOPSIS OF SUBSEQUENT CHAPTERS

This book provides practical examples of and reflections on campus-wide initiatives that bridge WAC and faculty development partnerships with diversity and inclusion initiatives. Chapter 1, "Faculty Development and Writing Across the Curriculum Initiatives: Enhancing Diversity in Twenty-First-Century Higher Education," reviews the ways in which both WAC and faculty development work have historically been connected in higher education, through both formal and informal structures. I also build on research that provides opportunities for collaborative partnerships through faculty development centers and WAC programs, by demonstrating the ways in which such collaborations can enhance diversity and inclusion initiatives at the institutional level. In essence, programmatic units can take stronger leadership and ownership over diversity and inclusion efforts when they work together.

In chapter 2, "Fostering Partnerships between WAC, Faculty Development, and Diversity and Inclusion in General Education Reform," I use Western Michigan University's general education reform process as an example to describe the ways that general education curricular revision provides ripe opportunities to strengthen collaboration between faculty development and WAC. This chapter further reflects on the successes and challenges associated with writing instruction when considering faculty development and WAC partnerships, while also addressing the ways in which diversity and inclusion and written communication student learning outcomes within general education programs can provide opportunities for workshops on assessment-based activities aligned with those student learning outcomes. Institutional assessment data one year after the launch of WMU's revised general education program are also analyzed.

In chapter 3, "The Work of Writing Never Ends: Writing Across the Curriculum and Diversity and Inclusion Professional Development Opportunities," I survey the existing literature on the ways in which centers for faculty development and teaching and learning and WAC programs have worked collaboratively through both formal, explicit partnerships and informal, implicit partnerships, where connections between writing and diversity intersect. This chapter further identifies specific opportunities and reasons for WAC programs and faculty development centers to form formal partnerships as they work collaboratively in a twenty-first-century context. Additionally, I will draw upon WMU's University College model of establishing the Merze Tate College. The Merze Tate College is named after the first African American woman to graduate from WMU, who also received her PhD from Harvard. Its namesake and foci strengthen and enhance diversity. Specific components of the Merze Tate College include a centralized model that merges student and career success, academic advising, WMU Essential Studies (general education), and the Writing Center under one centralized college that focuses on diversity, equity, and student enrollment. This chapter also draws from my experience designing both WAC and diversity and inclusion programming from OFD and in current administrative roles, to discuss how WAC and faculty development training and expertise help administrators, in particular college deans, craft large-scale leadership initiatives that assist with retention and student enrollment. Building on examples of programs created for WAC and faculty development, I describe the ways in which the work developed from these programs has shaped the institutional priorities that continue to address diversity and inclusion for faculty and students.

In chapter 4, "Toward an Institutional Transformation of WAC: A View Forward Despite Shrinking Operating Budgets," I review previous WAC scholarship on stand-alone WAC units that point to vulnerability for budget cuts in a post-COVID higher education context. In doing so, I urge readers to consider a new vision of WAC work, one that aligns more strongly with teaching and learning initiatives, and one that considers contributions to the broader field of faculty development, beyond rhetoric and composition scholarship. This chapter further describes the things I learned about institutional change once I began to do intellectual work outside of writing programs and academic departments, particularly at a time when my institution was experiencing multiple changes in senior leadership at the president, provost, and dean levels and when my institution began the process of moving from an incremental budget model, strategic resource management, to one that resembles responsibility-centered resource management (RCM). To effect long-term institutional change requires buy-in and support from senior-level administration, particularly at a time when state-funded institutions can no longer rely on state-supported funding primarily. For me, such change, however, would not have been possible without the grassroots efforts of faculty development centers in the absence of a WAC program.

I also draw from the discussion of the Merze Tate College model in chapter 4, in addition to WMUx, which now houses faculty development. Both fall under the purview of the Vice Provost for Teaching and Learning and are carefully integrated to foster stronger collaboration within and across units to enhance diversity, equity, and inclusion. In drawing upon this example, I argue that centralization, while threatening to individual unit identities, is the future of higher education. Leveraging centralization enables units to share resources, collaborations, and initiatives.

The final chapter, chapter 5, builds on the previous chapter by taking up key threats to WAC programs as stand-alone units. Using the process of centralization, especially as related to institutional budget models, enables us to connect the WAC, faculty development, and diversity and inclusion work with larger missions and initiatives that reflect institutional values. This, then, enables us to align our work with existing strategic plans. Collaborations with centralized units make visible the work that we do when stand-alone programs are threatened by budgetary constraints.

In sum, this book seeks to provide insights for those who direct or are looking to direct WAC programs, faculty developers who lead teaching and learning centers, and those interested in moving on to senior-level administrative positions beyond the department chair or WPA levels. Faculty developers take on a wide variety of roles including but not limited to directors of centers for teaching and learning (CTLs), instructional designers, and learning and teaching consultants and benefit greatly from the expertise of WPAs and WAC specialists. Likewise, WPAs and WAC specialists benefit greatly by gaining an in-depth understanding for how institutional change happens beyond the department or writing program. It is my sincerest hope that those with broad interests in higher education leadership and development, including directors of higher education leadership programs and university administrators (provosts, vice provosts, deans, and chairs or directors), will have a better understanding of the intellectual work that happens across institutional units and sites. Moreover, it is my sincerest hope that this book elevates conversations regarding institutional and programmatic change beyond work in writing program administration.

1

FACULTY DEVELOPMENT AND WRITING ACROSS THE CURRICULUM INITIATIVES

Enhancing Diversity in Twenty-First-Century Higher Education

In the introduction, I identified faculty development centers and WAC programs as opportunities to collaborate more explicitly on teaching and learning initiatives pertaining to the study of writing. Previous scholarship clearly affirms the roles that each plays with regard to professional development; however, in many circumstances, the degree to which both programs collaborate closely has not been detailed explicitly. Thus, I propose a formal relationship that links interest to the teaching of writing: I believe both faculty development and WAC programs can and should form formal collaborative partnerships in a commitment to enhancing diversity and inclusion practices at institutions of higher education. As discussed in the introduction, this book operates from the premise that (1) faculty development centers and WAC programs need to collaborate more formally and directly, and (2) this collaboration needs to make a strong commitment to diversity and inclusion missions of institutions of higher education.

In this chapter, I build on the previous literature surrounding faculty development work as offering potential opportunities to respond to calls for stronger diversity and inclusion initiatives in campus environments. In the first section of this chapter, I survey the literature on faculty development and diversity and inclusion initiatives. In the final section of this chapter, I identify areas of opportunity for diversity and inclusion programming centered around teaching inclusivity and ways that faculty development centers and WAC programs can participate in these efforts. In sum, these efforts serve as a foundational framework for making sense of the programming I've developed around diversity and inclusion as a writing specialist and faculty developer at WMU.

https://doi.org/10.7330/9781646424542.c001

FACULTY DEVELOPMENT DIVERSITY AND INCLUSION INITIATIVES

As discussed in *Creating the Future of Faculty Development*, a book that outlines the history and evolution of faculty development programming, the 1990s included a paradigm shift from faculty productivity to student learning. During this student learning era, faculty development programs began thinking more about student diversity needs in higher education (Sorcinelli, Austin, and Eddy 2006, 3–4). As a result, diversity was taken up with respect to multicultural initiatives to diversify teaching and learning methods for a more diverse student body, which encompassed a variety of "collaborative ventures" including but not limited to "improving general education . . . , attending to issues of gender, race, and class, and enhancing learning skills such as writing and critical thinking across the curriculum" (12). In chapter 3, I will discuss at length the roles of faculty development in relation to collaboration on general education and writing across the curriculum, and how each set of collaborative experiences can shape institutional commitments to diversity and inclusion.

Diversity initiatives are commonly identified programming areas of need in faculty development and teaching and learning centers. The sources referenced in this section point to an identified need for diversity while also acknowledging the progress toward diversity and inclusion that is still needed. As Mathew L. Ouellett contends, "Although colleges and universities may herald diversity and inclusion as cherished values, they have yet to make sufficient institutional progress toward the aspirational goal of access for all to excellence in teaching and learning" (2004, 136). He further argues that as a result of these gaps, "faculty development must contribute to the creation of a pipeline for staffing of teaching and learning centers by encouraging the recruitment and mentoring for faculty developers who are sensitive to a range of diversity issues, willing to incorporate new pedagogical models" (144). While published in 2004, Ouellett's scholarship is consistent with ensuing work around diversity and faculty development programming.

Ouellett's overview of faculty development programming in Kay J. Gillespie and Douglas L. Robertson's *Guide to Faculty Development* (2010a) further identifies diversity as one of four key topics of "universal concern" for faculty developers and instructional designers (9). Ouellett later notes that while faculty developers have paid attention to organizational structures since the 1970s, "what has been neglected is how deeply diversity and multicultural dynamics embed these issues at every level of our practice" (13). In response to this neglect, Ouellett references Marchesani and Jackson's theory of multicultural organizational development (MCOD) as a method for designing social justice and diversity goals at institutions of higher education, noting that MCOD can help achieve diversity and social justice goals by targeting systemic and institutional change (13). Of MCOD, Ouellett determines that

> unlike other organizational change systems, in the MCOD model a level of social justice must be present in order to pursue social diversity. [Faculty development] would benefit from an expansion of research paradigms to include data-driven multicultural organization development models in order to expand our understanding of the unique contributions and challenges in different institutional settings, such as community colleges, Historically Black Colleges and Universities (HBCUs), predominately [*sic*] Hispanic Serving Institutions (HSIs), and Tribal Colleges. (13)

Ouellett's chapter concludes by arguing that faculty development would benefit tremendously from diverse initiatives and charges faculty developers to devote critical attention to bringing diverse groups of faculty, programming, support, and resources to assist faculty with meeting institutional needs (14–15).

Existing scholarship readily identifies the need to increase diversity programming. One strategy for achieving progress is through not only increasing faculty development programming around diversity but also purposefully targeting institutional change more broadly and directly. In the chapter "Nurturing Institutional Change: Collaboration and Leadership between Upper Level Administrators and Faculty Developers," Devorah Lieberman (2012) identifies the faculty developer's role as essential to shaping the teaching and learning practices associated with institutionally aligned diversity and inclusion initiatives, noting: "It is important that faculty development staff be nimble and able to be considered 'go-to' professionals who can address needs from the perspective of the individual faculty member or administrator, a department or other institutional unit, or the college or university as a whole" (67–68). Moreover, within this role as the "go-to" person, Lieberman further contends that it is essential for faculty development to be "embedded into specific program initiatives to advance institutional change" (69).

Lieberman then identifies several institutional models for effective change; such models serve as a "blueprint" for successful programming and faculty development activities. Examples of diversity-related programming and activities are offered as part of this blueprint, and include international diversity training for faculty and staff, diversity action councils, support for implementing diversity in first-year courses and curricula, and action council luncheons and events (69). While many campuses across US higher education include diversity components, what is important to emphasize here is the official role of faculty development in creating and developing specific programs around diversity and inclusion, ones that are strategically aligned with the institution's mission.

At the end of her chapter, Lieberman provides six principles for positioning faculty developers as the change agents for the institution because the work of faculty developers shapes and has "a dramatic impact on the central role of most colleges and universities" (70). Of the six principles identified in the chapter, the one that resonates most for the purposes of this chapter is the need to place faculty development centers "close to the heart of campus" (70), preferably close to the provost or president's office. As a rationale, Lieberman asserts that close physical or geographical proximity "communicates metaphorical proximity to the mission of the institution" (70). Given the central role of faculty development in effecting institutional change, it is meaningful that Lieberman's chapter touches on diversity and inclusion initiatives while offering specific models and examples.

Ouellett (2010b) similarly connects diversity and inclusion initiatives with systemic and institutional change in ways that align with the broader mission of postsecondary institutions. In his assessment of institutional progress toward diversity, he states the following:

> Today, as faculty developers realize the importance of systemic change efforts that span the organization and link to central institutional and civic goals (Milem, Chang, and Antonio, 2005), they seek initiatives to align strategic efforts by students, instructors, campus leaders, and communities with multicultural and diversity-related goals (Hurtado et al., 1999; Marchesani and Jackson, 2005). (186)

Ouellett moreover indicates that such efforts reflect interests in recruiting and retaining both diverse student bodies and diverse faculty profiles, but our understandings of what diverse profiles look like continue to evolve, reflecting increasingly complex understandings of what precisely is meant by "diversity" (186–87). Expansion in the area continues to evolve as institutions implement initiatives that respond to diversity and inclusion efforts. Many of these initiatives include more specific accounts of the experiences of faculty and students of historically oppressed populations, increased efforts to provide support for underrepresented minorities at predominantly white institutions (PWIs), and hiring and creating diversity chief officer positions (187). For Ouellett, faculty developers must play a role in these institutional endeavors.

Additional scholarship identifies how essential it is that faculty developers communicate and work directly with senior administration when collaborating on diversity and inclusion initiatives. While faculty developers maintain a critical role when providing professional development on diversity and inclusion for faculty members regarding teaching and learning practices, the ways in which they work, collaborate, and communicate with administrators contain some key differences. Todd D. Zakrajsek (2010) states:

> The biggest difference is that faculty members will primarily want to know what can be provided to help them as individuals, and administrators will primarily want to know what can be provided to help the institution . . . For example, a vice president for diversity is responsible for the way in which the entire faculty perceives and interacts with individuals from a variety of underrepresented groups. This vice president may want to know how to present information effectively to faculty members, but [they are] probably more interested in assistance in achieving the overall diversity goals of the institution. (92)

When considering the role of change agents, institutional change is often long-term and larger-scale. Because institutional change often takes time, it is critical that faculty development initiatives align with a university's vision or mission, statements that are often designed by institutions to reflect a range of years and actionable items. Working on long-range projects with administrators should not be done at the expense of neglecting the day-to-day needs of faculty with regard to diverse teaching and learning practices, though. Thus, the faculty developer must balance both long-term and short-term needs as change agents, especially when working directly on sustaining diversity and inclusion initiatives.

Institutional buy-in, especially from senior-level administrators, is key to effecting change, especially when engaging diversity and inclusion initiatives (Kiyama, Lee, and Rhoades 2012, 281). Furthermore, having a campus that is committed to both diversity and cross-unit collaborations is also critical to transforming institutional practices. In one example of institutional practices and models, Adrianna Kezar (2006) identifies the faculty development center as a potential "secondary or complementary center on campus for cross-unit work . . ." (820). In addition to the faculty development center are collaborations, usually through offices of the president as the centralized unit of collaboration (820). At one institution identified in her study, Kezar identifies study participants interviewed who were able to "recite the areas of collaborative work—diversity, internationalization, student support, and assessment—as well as their contribution and involvement in these efforts" (820). Similar to Lieberman's discussion is the idea that faculty development centers play critical roles as change agents, as they collaborate on diversity-related initiatives that align with the mission of institutions and their leadership.

Diversity and inclusion clearly represent opportunities for faculty developers to serve as change agents on their campuses. More precise empirical data indicate diversity and inclusion as an increased opportunity for growth in the areas of faculty and organizational development. Beach and colleagues' (2016) most recent study reveals that from their own survey of faculty development directors,

> multiculturalism and diversity related to teaching [were] identified by 15% of the directors for expansion across most institutional types . . . In comprehensive institutions, 21% of directors support expanding this focus. At community colleges, 23% of directors support expansion. Recognition is growing that the challenges facing this country and broader international community require the talents of the full range of the population. Enhanced attention to programs that support multiculturalism and diversity in regard to teaching and learning processes is likely to stay on the horizon for directors as they establish priorities for moving forward. (45)

Along the lines of alignment with an institution's mission is the necessity to identify faculty development initiatives pertaining to diversity and inclusion as a priority, one that requires support. Clearly, a range of directors identify the necessity for designing diversity and inclusion programming, and the authors determined that based on these findings, institutional needs for diversity and inclusion programming will continue well into the twenty-first century as campus enrollment demographics continue to shift toward a more multicultural student body. That said, these findings also reveal increased opportunities for growth with respect to diversity and inclusion priorities since the majority of faculty development directors surveyed did not identify diversity and inclusion as an area of expansion. The question remains as to why more directors did not identify diversity and inclusion as a potential area of expansion. To be fair, there may well be some legitimate obstacles shaping the ways in which respondents answered the question, with limited resources being an obvious rationale. Another possible reason might be that respondents consider existing diversity programming as sufficient and therefore already meeting institutional needs. Nonetheless, if faculty developers are to play key roles as change agents, then contributing to diversity and inclusion in ways that align with the missions of many of our postsecondary institutions should be an explicit priority.

Perhaps the final reason why most directors did not identify diverse programming as opportunities for expansion can be explained by a limited representation of diversity among faculty developers. As Beach and colleagues note, "Faculty developers, however, are predominantly aging, White, and female, a profile that does not align with the demographics of the overall faculty" (55). Despite the issue of limited representation, Beach and coauthors do consider diversity and inclusion as integral to the work of faculty developers, and they also are clear about opportunities for organizations and faculty developers to make stronger commitments toward advancing diversity and inclusion. They acknowledge that POD Network (Professional and Organizational Development Network), the flagship organization for faculty developers, affirms their commitment to increasing diversity and inclusion among faculty developers represented both on campuses and within the POD Network as an organization, noting:

> Through the POD Network, those in the field of faculty development have made concerted efforts to actively pursue a more diverse membership, including the establishment of a diversity committee, diversity grants, and joint meetings . . . with the members of the POD Network and the HBCU Faculty development network. The outcomes of these efforts are yet to be realized. The data suggest that Native Americans / American Indians, Asian / Pacific Islanders, and Black African Americans remain but a fraction of faculty developers in the POD Network. (28)

To be clear, I understand diversity encompasses a much broader understanding of demographics beyond race, and Beach and coauthors' discussion does touch on age and gender representations among faculty developers, therefore suggesting a broader understanding of representation beyond race. The points to emphasize, however, are that (1) diversity efforts have been identified as opportunities for expansion among some respondents, and (2) POD as an organization has determined that additional work with regard to diversity expansion needs to be done to enhance the organization's mission and values, which include diversity, inclusion, and social justice advocacy among many others (POD Network, n.d.).

While the limited representation of diverse faculty developers poses a challenge, Beach and colleagues' profile of faculty development and teaching and learning centers does identify significant institutional profiles of centers with diversity and inclusion programming and initiatives. One example includes Duquesne University's Center of Teaching Excellence (CTE), which advocates social justice and cross-cultural pedagogies. Duquesne's CTE "weaves" their focus on cross-cultural and social justice pedagogies across a variety of faculty development programming, including "workshops, panel discussions, online references, and resources offered through the campus library" (Beach et al. 2016,

45). One of their specific workshops, "Exploring Race and Pedagogy at Our Predominantly White University," focuses on pedagogical practices designed to improve learning outcomes among underrepresented minority groups (45). I highlight this example of a workshop because it affirms a commitment to diversity despite limited representation among historically oppressed populations at the institution. While increasing representation among faculty and faculty developers is one way to achieve diversity, it is also important for faculty developers to maintain a commitment to diverse teaching practices regardless of the demographics and representations among faculty and faculty developers.

In sum, the body of literature discussed in this section simply scratches the surface with respect to faculty development diversity and inclusion efforts. The most compelling takeaways involve an increased commitment to diversity and inclusion across the landscape of higher education, and the need for faculty developers to play a role as change agents to transform diversity and inclusion efforts on college campuses. In chapter 5, I will identify a few faculty development models for diversity and inclusion that have shaped the work I've done as a faculty developer.

WAC PROGRAMMING, DIVERSITY, AND INCLUSION

WAC programming has always been foundational to effecting institutional change. As Tiffany Rousculp (2021) writes: "As 'one of the longest running educational reform movements in higher education in the U.S.' (INWAC 2014), [WAC] began in response to increasing and diversifying student populations and was based upon knowledges of writing and learning that were developed in the early 1970s . . ." (107). Elaine P. Maimon's preface in Susan H. McLeod and Margot Soven's collection, *Writing Across the Curriculum: A Guide to Developing Programs*, identifies the critical role of WAC programming in fulfilling commitments to diversity and inclusion. She writes:

> Writing across the curriculum means incorporating student responses into teaching. When we take student responses into account, we give new meaning to teaching for diversity. When classrooms in all disciplines focus on writing as a process of self-discovery and as a means for social interaction, we are really attending to the voices of diversity in our classes. (2000, ix–x)

Put simply, the very nature of WAC outreach lends itself to enhancing diversity, because incorporating writing within all disciplines provides institutions with a wider range of student abilities and identities, something that few disciplines can offer alone. It also allows various fields of study to see how writing is indeed a social act (Bazerman 1994; Brodkey 1987; Russell 1997), permitting self-discovery, civic engagement, and responsibility.

Christopher Thaiss's (2000) discussion in the same collection further identifies the relevance of WAC, especially with regard to general education reform. Thaiss contends that the goals of general education have traditionally been too idealistic (i.e., enhancing cultural diversity), while the skills necessary for those entering majors and preprofessional careers are too narrowly defined (71). Thaiss argues that the very fact that these curricula goals are positioned so widely apart makes it increasingly difficult for WAC programmers to plan relevant workshops. Thaiss writes:

> But because such curricula emerge out of debate of widely differing positions, and because the courses, whatever their shape on paper, will be taught by diverse people with diverse agendas, every general education program has lots of room for experimentation. This makes general education fun for the WAC planner, and indicates a workshop design that promotes imaginative thinking and a multitude of individual plans. (71)

Read in this light, diversity programming is positioned as a liability and not an enhancement. In other words, providing programming so that writing assignments can be designed effectively for general education courses with broader arching goals like enhancing cultural diversity, while also providing sufficient programming for majors with specific accreditation requirements and prescribed professional conventions, poses specific challenges for WAC developers and specialists who must meet the needs and expectations of both audiences. That said, Thaiss does acknowledge a few solutions to meet the needs of both audiences (74); however, given current assaults on liberal arts education in conjunction with state legislative shifts to vocational/trade skill sets (Lind 2006), I am concerned that commitments to diversity could potentially disappear, especially when promoting WAC outreach, if institutions do not create partnerships more diligently and purposefully. Unsurprisingly, most of the discussion in Mcleod and Soven's collection, as it pertains to diversity, focuses exclusively on diverse and social justice writing assignments in general education courses (see, e.g., Graham 2000) outside of Maimon's discussion in the preface. In short, while general education affords initial opportunities to engage WAC and diversity topics, it is important for WAC and diversity collaborations to extend beyond core curricula.

More recently, scholars like Chris Anson (2012) argue that topics of diversity have lagged far behind in terms of WAC outreach, especially when considering the breadth of scholarship on race more broadly in rhetoric and composition research and scholarship. Anson suggests, more specifically, that racial diversity has not been addressed at length in WAC scholarship, noting missed opportunities to tap into work "from theories of racial identity in the classroom to the conundrum of dialect and style differences in student work. WAC has especially lagged behind in helping scholars, administrators and teachers across a broad range of disciplines to implement best practices in assessing the writing of diverse learners, both at the classroom and programmatic levels" (15). It is also worth noting that Anson's contribution is the only mention of WAC in the collection *Race and Writing Assessment*, edited by Asao B. Inoue and Mya Poe, thus reinforcing the lack of attention WAC has traditionally been paid when considering race and writing assessment practices.

Specifically speaking of the relationships between WAC and faculty development partnerships on diversity and inclusion initiatives, recent scholarship has pointed to developments in anti-racist workshops and social justice, particularly as connected to both linguistic justice and LGBTQ+ rights (Borboa-Peterson, Ozaki, and Kelsch 2021; Martini and Webster 2021). Borboa and coauthors provide one concrete example of what happens when faculty development directors, diversity and inclusion administrators, and writing across the curriculum directors collaborate in pursuit of social justice, noting:

> For example, when the director of faculty development (situated in our teaching center) began working with the director of student diversity and inclusion (situated in student affairs) this also meant a connection between the coordinator of the university writing program (who does faculty development work through writing across the curriculum) and the senior program coordinator for LGBTQ+ and cross-cultural programming (working within the office of student diversity and inclusion). Our conversations led us to gaps in knowledge and skill on the academic side that offered a venue to draw in the student affairs side to share their expertise and insights. (10)

The previous quotation sums up precisely why collaborations between each of these units is essential to fulfill higher education's mission toward diversity and inclusion. In subsequent chapters, I identify each of the contributions between faculty development and WAC toward making diversity and inclusion work a reality and not simply an aspiration.

CONCLUSION

Scholarship in both faculty development and WAC indicates a necessity to develop programming that focuses on diversity and inclusion initiatives. While both sets of scholarship consider these necessities, formal collaboration and partnerships around diversity are limited: faculty development data and research include desires for more diversity programming, while limited attention has been paid to diversity more generally within WAC programming. While writing centers have performed much of the faculty development labor, especially in the absence of formal WAC programs, writing centers often lack the institutional resources to build formal professional development programming exclusively for faculty (Isaacs and Knight 2014). By uniting both faculty development centers and WAC programs, institutions have additional opportunities to design and develop diversity and inclusion programming, as both audiences have much to contribute and offer one another. Faculty development centers offer longer-term and sustained programming for complex topics such as diversity; they also provide WAC specialists with additional opportunities to consider diverse teaching and learning practices beyond linguistic diversity. By the same token, WAC specialists offer faculty development centers sophisticated understandings of rhetorical knowledge and versatility, foundational knowledge that potentially connects what we know about rhetoric and cultural rhetorics with audiences outside of our discipline. In effect, both faculty development centers and WAC programs possess the capacity to reach wider audiences through purposeful and explicit partnerships and collaborations.

The next chapter describes and reflects on my experiences with curriculum revision and the implications for both WAC and diversity and inclusion work. Further, I share examples of ways that we may leverage contributions between the two to foster stronger partnerships and collaborations through faculty development, particularly with general education reform. Such partnerships have provided opportunities to include diversity and inclusion student learning outcomes within a general education program.

2

FOSTERING PARTNERSHIPS BETWEEN WAC, FACULTY DEVELOPMENT, AND DIVERSITY AND INCLUSION IN GENERAL EDUCATION REFORM

My participation in WMU's general education reform began unexpectedly. Upon obtaining tenure in the Department of English and while still directing the First-Year Writing program, I learned from our department's Faculty Senate representative that a committee had been appointed to reform general education. From the representative I learned that every course would need to be recertified in accordance with a newly revised model that could potentially repeal the first-year writing requirement at WMU, should the revised model no longer include first-year writing or should it redistribute writing instruction across various colleges and academic units outside of English. Upon learning of these threats, I inquired about the possibility of joining the Faculty Senate Ad Hoc Committee on General Education. My chief purpose was to simply stop the committee from doing away with a first-year writing requirement or outsourcing the labor of writing instruction to those who possess no training or expertise. Little did I know that my role would shift from protecting first-year writing toward making the case for WAC and faculty development resources and for supporting assisting faculty and instructors in revising and designing new general education courses.

This chapter, then, traces my journey through general education reform at WMU. This journey examines four primary phases of participation in general education reform. With the first phase, the Ad Hoc Committee in General Education, I reflect on the committee's work, including its self-study on general education and its charge to design new learning outcomes for the general education program. With the second phase, the Ad Hoc Committee Design Team, the team charged with identifying a new name and curricular model for generation education based on previously approved learning outcomes, I reflect on

https://doi.org/10.7330/9781646424542.c002

the processes and challenges associated with advocating the necessities of WAC outreach and support based on the proposed and approved curricular model, which included multiple writing-intensive courses. With the third phase, the Ad Hoc Logistics Committee, I reflect on my contributions associated with the committee's charges to identify logistical concerns and resources, include recommendations for an implementation plan, and identify necessary resources for implementation. It was with the third phase that my role as faculty developer became crucial to the work of that committee. Further, it was within this phase that I began to understand my role with faculty development as central to the contributions I made while serving on the Ad Hoc Logistics Committee.

The final phase, the WMU Essential Studies (WES) Executive Advisory Committee, concluded the formation of the committee that oversees WMU's general education program, WMU Essential Studies. My analysis of this phase includes a reflection on and discussion of the opportunities that WMU Essential Studies has had to collaborate with OFD on developing workshops to support faculty with designing new WES courses, submitting WES courses for approval, and submitting assessment plans for assessing student learning outcomes, including written communication and diversity and inclusion outcomes. I offer WES as one example of how WAC and faculty development collaborations designed around diversity and inclusion can lead to institutional change and progress.

With each phase of general education reform, it became increasingly clear that WAC and faculty development centers play critical roles in an institution's commitment to revising general education. Moreover, in this chapter I argue not only that WAC and faculty development centers have key roles in institutions' commitments to general education, but also that the contributions that both kinds of programs or centers make with respect to general education become greatly enhanced when WAC and faculty development centers work directly and collaboratively. Through my roles as both a WPA and faculty developer and as associate and acting dean, I have worked to develop specific WAC faculty development programming in an institutional space that houses no official WAC program. As such, I present WAC outreach under the auspices of a faculty development center as one model for fostering stronger and more direct connections between WAC and faculty development centers. Based on these experiences, I have found that productivity is enhanced to move general education reform forward.

THE ROLE OF FACULTY DEVELOPMENT AND
WAC IN GENERAL EDUCATION REFORM

Prior to reflecting on the three phases of general education reform, it is first important to provide a brief discussion that reviews the roles of faculty development and WAC programs in general education. When tracing the evolution of faculty development centers, Sorcinelli, Austin, and Eddy (2006) identify the key roles of faculty development centers when institutions begin widespread curricular reform, because such reforms cannot "be addressed by individual faculty members" alone (12). They also identify both general education reform and WAC movements as opportunities for faculty developers to provide support for faculty in designing courses, establishing course goals, and identifying course outcomes for assessment (12). In addition, their discussion is consistent with Jerry Gaff and Ronald D. Simpson's (1994), who also conclude, "For each of these agendas, faculty development became the means to the end of curriculum change . . . Faculty development for curricular change required groups of faculty to work together to see their own individual interest within the context of the department or institution" (170).

Interestingly, while Sorcinelli and coauthors also acknowledge the significance of general education reform as it connects to faculty development, and while they also point to "new ideas and trends [that] include increased attention to the interrelation of general education and the major, to the teaching and learning process, and to global and domestic diversity," their own survey of respondents indicated that "faculty developers did not identify [general education] as one for which they currently offered programming in any significant way, nor did they rate the issue as a particularly important focus for programming" (91). As possible explanations for this finding, Sorcinelli and colleagues point to the facts that general education reform often falls under administrative leadership and not a faculty development office; that reform often is handled at program, course, or institutional levels; and that general education reform often focuses on content and not on "strategies for teaching and learning" (91). As readers will see, later in this chapter I discuss how general education reform at WMU in fact pointed to needs related to teaching and learning, because the revised model shifted the focus from course content and distributions toward the creation of a foundational set of skills that students and instructors should apply to course content. That shift, then, provoked conversations about the role of faculty development in assisting instructors with teaching and learning strategies to teach skills in relation to content. Furthermore, because writing is identified as an essential learning outcome and foundational skill at WMU, faculty would need WAC support to teach writing in relation to their content areas of expertise. Such facts cosign my argument that faculty development centers and WAC programs must form explicit partnerships as they work collaboratively.

With reference to teaching and learning strategies, Gillespie and Robertson's (2010) collection, *A Guide to Faculty Development*, further examines the roles of faculty development in general education reform. Virginia S. Lee's contribution identifies faculty learning communities (FLC), facilitated by faculty development centers as key players in general education reform (28). She further identifies faculty development centers as key partners in assessment practices associated with general education reform (31). Constance Ewing Cook and Michele Marincovich's chapter, "Effective Practices at Research Universities: The Productive Pairing of Research and Teaching," also references the role of faculty development centers in designing general education, specifically in the case of learning communities housed under the auspices of Harvard's Derek Bok Center for Teaching and Learning (278).

A key role for faculty development centers also includes the necessity of providing professional development in relation to assessment when considering general education. In "Assessment Practices to Student Learning: Transformative Assessment," Catherine M. Wehlburg (2010) states that "as part of an ongoing faculty development program, many institutions encourage faculty to list outcomes for general education or for the major on the course syllabus. Faculty developers can help to create curriculum maps to determine how a specific course fits into the overall departmental or program learning" (175). Also, Kathryn M. Plank and Alan Kalish reference Walvoord's best practices in assessment and general education as they pertain to faculty development (2010, 137–38), noting: "Particularly important for faculty development is the principle of integration. In order for the outcomes of an assessment to tell a coherent story, it is important to treat one's practice as multidimensional and integrated and to be able to demonstrate the connections across seemingly disparate areas of service" (138).

Another compelling theme from Gillespie and Robertson's collection is the role of interrelated faculty development, general education, and career training. Helen Burnstad and Cynthia J. Hoss's chapter, "Faculty Development in the Context of the Community College," discusses the ways in which faculty development centers can help instructors make connections between general education courses and students' prospective careers. Of faculty development centers, they assert the following:

> Hence, faculty development efforts need to be framed around the development and use of these strategies with students. Since so many community college faculty members teach in career programs and general education courses that support career programs, they need to be prepared to support students pursuing these career paths. Faculty choices are important in helping students learn workplace skills, and faculty members are vital in aiding students to enhance *critical thinking, writing ability, mathematical reasoning, and information literacy skills.* To that end, faculty development usually supports each faculty member in learning how to use and evaluate assignments to be more effective in learning communities. (2010, 314; emphasis added).

In addition to the essential roles of faculty development centers, it is important to emphasize the ways that faculty development centers can help instructors reinforce skills that students need to perform successfully in their careers. This is critical, because it positions general education away from content with which students may or may not be engaged toward the skills students need to be successful in a twenty-first-century context. I also emphasize specific sets of skills identified, including critical thinking, writing, quantitative reasoning, and information literacy, because as readers will see later in this chapter, these sets of skills were identified as foundational skill course requirements in WMU's revised general education model. Moreover, such an emphasis on skill is consistent with the shift from content to skill development in WMU's general education reform.

While skill-building and faculty development are often emphasized in general education reform, WAC has historically taken on a smaller role. In "WAC and General Education Courses," Christopher Thaiss (2000) indicates:

> Because of larger class sizes and because of relative lack of attention paid by full-time faculties to the general education courses in universities, examples of WAC programs focused on general education and core curricula are fewer than those of programs centered on the major, most commonly in writing-intensive courses. These tendencies create difficulties for WAC planners, but it is these tendencies that make writing so important a tool in general education. (63)

Put simply, WAC is often seen as a key—but often untapped—resource for contributing to professional development for faculty teaching in general education core curriculum, because general education courses can potentially include Writing to Learn activities for discovery, even in courses with large class sizes. In terms of WAC programming that targets teaching writing in a student's major, such professional development can help students understand and produce the written conventions associated with their majors or prospective careers. In contrast, with general education, there is an opportunity to help students discover knowledge through writing. I would also add, though, that general education courses help students make connections between the conventions associated with writing in various content courses and how those conventions differ across subject areas and academic disciplines. Beyond first-year writing, general education also provides campuses with a critical opportunity to understand how writing shapes and impacts the knowledge they acquire and generate; it also helps students make connections across courses.

Another argument for understanding the value of writing in general education curricula is based on the fact that writing as an activity shows students the usefulness of a general education curricula, particularly since most general education courses are those which students do not want to take (Thaiss 2000, 64). Thaiss further contends: "If faculties genuinely believe in the usefulness of the general education requirements, then they need to find ways to (1) help see the work as meaningful and (2) include definite choices that students can make within the course structure. Writing can help bring about both objectives" (64). Such an argument is especially useful for WMU's institutional context, because the revised model seeks to make general education more useful by helping students understand how skills acquired from foundational courses can be applied to content-based courses. Writing as an activity also helps students articulate their understandings of course objectives and, in essence, provides faculty with a potential tool for assessing these outcomes. Hence, the shift from gaining familiarity to a wide range of content subjects toward understanding skills as tools that can be used to engage content-based study enables students to see more tangibly the value of general education. Moreover, writing is positioned front and center when considering the most salient skills faculty desire for students to acquire in higher education.

Thaiss's chapter also provides some tangible examples of what WAC has to offer in terms of professional development of faculty teaching general education courses. These include examples of writing assignments (65), feedback and responding to student writing when considering larger class sizes (66–67), understanding the writing process (68), evaluating student writing (69), and participating in academic learning communities (70), to name a few. While not an exhaustive list, these ideas provide possibilities for what WAC programs can offer in terms of professional development, often through the workshop model; leveraging partnerships with faculty development centers provides increased opportunities to meet faculties' instructional professional development needs.

More recent scholarship emphasizes the value of WAC professional development for faculty teaching general education, though this role remains smaller in comparison to the role of WAC in teaching students to write in specific majors. In "A Taxonomy of Writing Across the Curriculum Programs: Evolving to Serve Broader Agendas," William Condon and Carol Ruiz (2012) acknowledge previous scholarship that points to threats that a focus on WAC in general education will "cut WAC off from the disciplines" (357; also see Jones and Comprone 1993, 61). Condon and Ruiz also acknowledge that "WAC can be attractive to faculties as a means of delivering general education or first-year seminars, yet WAC writ large delivers much greater benefits to curriculum and to students' learning than such narrow conceptions would allow" (358). That said, their taxonomy identifies established WAC programs as those that have their own identity, as distinguished from "general education or other allies" (362).

While desirable for WAC to have its own organizational identity, it is the latter emphasis on "other allies" that may potentially reinforce silos, limiting collaborations with campus-wide teaching and learning centers. Condon and Ruiz later reference Carleton College's Writing Program as a recipient of the "Exemplary Program Award for 2010 from the Association for General and Liberal Studies," an award that recognizes their "role in collaboration among faculty for assessment and pedagogy in the service of general education" (379). Such recognition potentially makes space for WAC and faculty development centers to serve as possible locations for collaboration on assessment and general education. In addition to Carleton College, Condon and Ruiz also describe Washington State University as another example for collaboration on WAC work, including formal partnerships formed through their Office of Undergraduate Education, General Education program, and their center for teaching and learning, now named the Office of Innovation and Assessment (376). What is also significant from this example is the fact that their center for teaching and learning had previously partnered with their WAC program in the past. Additional recent scholarship maintains this emphasis on opportunities for WAC and general education collaboration. In their historical account for the evolution of WAC outreach, Rowena Harper and Karen Orr Vered (2017) state that WAC or WID (writing in the disciplines) is often integrated in general education curricular requirements and indicate that a commitment to professional development for faculty is one of the ways that WAC and WID programs are distinguished from other support services across campuses of higher education (696).

Based on previously referenced scholarship in this section, both faculty development centers and WAC programs have key roles in providing professional development for faculty who teach general education courses, though interests in general education remain less explored in both areas. In the next section of this chapter, I explain how I've leveraged my experiences as a WPA, a member of general education reform committees, and faculty developer as an opportunity to increase the amount of attention and professional development offered for faculty and instructors who teach general education. As such, I will trace my journey through the three phases of general education reform.

GENERAL EDUCATION SELF-STUDY AND THE ROLE OF WPAS

The context and rationale for reforming general education at WMU was in response to a recent 2010 visit from the Higher Learning Commission (HLC), who determined that WMU was not adequately assessing its general education program. There were no clear learning outcomes for the program, and it was unclear how faculty were assessing the skills and knowledge students gained upon completing the program and graduating. Thus, in 2013 the Faculty Senate appointed an Ad Hoc Committee on General Education to complete a self-study on WMU's general education program. The committee included faculty, administrators, staff, academic advisors, "and representatives from the Office for Sustainability, Student Affairs, University Relations, the Office of Faculty Development, and First-Year Experience" (Faculty Senate, 2016, iv). The committee's self-study included focus groups with faculty and students, a descriptive analysis of current general education offerings, and specific recommendations for general education reform, recommendations that would be voted on and approved by the Faculty Senate. More specific committee charges were to:

- Examine Western Michigan University's current general education program in light of recent innovations in such programs around the country in order to determine if changes should be recommended. The committee may want to consider findings from the Association of American Colleges and Universities and programs at similar institutions that have been described as innovative and effective.
- Examine the learning outcomes that should be addressed by the general education program. This includes an examination of WMU's current outcomes and those of other innovative programs.
- Recommend ways in which to better integrate the general education learning outcomes across disciplines and curricula.
- Recommend ways in which to help students appreciate the goals of the general education program.

- Recommend a system by which the general education program can
  be assessed with the purpose of continual improvement. (iv)

Key findings from the report revealed significant dissatisfaction with the
current general education program, a program that had not been revised in more than thirty-five years. Examples of dissatisfaction included
a lack of understanding and purpose around general education, with
many focus groups also expressing dissatisfaction with a name as generic
and vague as "general education" might suggest; lack of communication
about the purposes and benefits associated with general education; and
the lack of connections between general education courses, students'
majors, and students' professional goals (1).

Based on these findings the committee made the following recommendations to the Faculty Senate:

- "endorse a learner-centered approach," in alignment with with
  WMU's mission, that identifies key skills and content necessary of
  students to learn in a twenty-first-century higher education context;
- adopt university-wide essential learning outcomes for the general
  education program;
- adopt a curriculum that supports these learning outcomes, one that
  builds on foundational skills and knowledge, applies these skills and
  knowledge to content areas using "big questions" or "real-world"
  applications, and enhances students' work with majors and minors,
  while also providing capstone experiences, and connects across units
  and initiatives on campus;
- provides ongoing assessment to address concerns from the afore-
  mentioned HLC report; and
- appoints a design team that develops alternative models for the
  revised general education program and recommends a new name
  for general education. (iv)

My participation on the Ad Hoc Committee on General Education
began after most of the self-study data were gathered; I assisted with
completing the final report that made recommendations to the Faculty
Senate. As previously stated, my service on WMU's Ad Hoc Committee
on General Education was intended to prevent the committee from
doing away with the first-year writing requirement or outsourcing writing instruction to other units; as WPA it was my prime commitment to
protect the First-Year Writing program and its value to the University.
In fall 2015, I received an email from the English Department's faculty senator explaining that the Faculty Senate would be discussing
the committee's progress on general education reform. The faculty
senator shared with the department that WMU was designing a new
general education program and model, that all courses would have

to be certified and justified, and that the model would be designed to shift away from teaching content in isolation to teaching skills across a variety of different departments. Based on my interpretation of this report, I concluded that courses like first-year writing were vulnerable, since an emphasis on content might suggest that writing courses would be taught in content areas and not exclusively in a first-year writing program, where training is required to teach such courses. Further, this proposed plan seemed like an opportunity for departments to grab extra credit hours through required courses, appropriate for an environment like WMU where college and department funding models are driven by course enrollment. I had also been privy to discussions across colleges about teaching skills outside of arts and sciences. There had been stories about how schools of nursing thought they could teach Spanish for nurses as opposed to nursing students taking classes in the Department of Spanish. Within this institutional context, writing courses seemed vulnerable since many still believe that anyone can teach writing, and since WMU has no current WAC programmatic structure to provide training and professional development for faculty teaching writing.

Thus, I joined the committee to make the case for having a first-year writing course prior to teaching skills in the content areas. I argued that students would need foundational knowledge and skills before applying them to specialized areas. Fortunately, the committee agreed and shared that there was never a concerted plan to do away with first-year writing. Later in this chapter, I will describe the general education model, now called WMU Essential Studies, that shows how students would take a three-level sequence of courses that begins with foundational skills-based courses that are applied to specialized areas of study. In addition to another colleague who also joined the committee to make the case for oral communication as a foundational skill, I also argued that it was too early to identify courses and models without adopting specific learning outcomes for the program first. Thus, discussions about certifying courses were premature. As a committee, we decided to identify essential learning outcomes for the program, from which a design team could present alternative models that align with them. It was at this phase, then, that we identified that upon completion of the general education requirements, students would be able to do the following:

a. Expand their understanding of human cultures and the physical/natural world
   • Increase their foundational knowledge of the sciences, social sciences, humanities and the arts

- Apply different methods of intellectual inquiry, investigation, and discovery
- Develop awareness of how everyday actions affect quality of life for all

b. Enhance intellectual and practical skills
- Demonstrate effective and appropriate oral, written, and digital communication abilities
- Develop creative and critical thinking
- Demonstrate and apply information and scientific literacy
- Analyze and interpret quantitative data

c. Exercise personal and social responsibility
- Develop understanding and practices for personal wellness
- Develop sensitivity to diversity and inclusion
- Exercise civic responsibility and become engaged in their communities at the local level and beyond
- Develop global and international perspectives
- Gain familiarity with a language other than English and/or the culture associated with it
- Develop practices for planetary sustainability

d. Exhibit integrative and applied learning
- Apply ethical, critical informed thought within and across disciplines
- Work both independently and collaboratively with others to achieve goals
- Become lifelong learners. (WMU Faculty Senate 2016)

While as a committee we wrote learning outcomes that reflected the skills, knowledge, and values we wanted students to gain across disciplines, it is noteworthy that many of the conversations we had both as a committee and with faculty focus groups centered around written communication and critical thinking. What is also interesting is how the conversations about writing are also focused on the desires of faculty to teach writing well. Of course, there were those "why Johnny can't write" conversations; however, for me it was one of the first occasions to see faculty admitting the responsibilities they bear to teach writing well. Moreover, I was also surprised that conversations about credit hour production and the grab for resources to teach writing within the departments did not occur at this phase, though those conversations and concerns about how departments in the arts and sciences were vulnerable to preprofessional colleges did eventually occur. This phase perhaps reflected the least resistance for faculty buy-in on general education reform (much different from the latter phase, to be described in this chapter). This phase did, nonetheless, reinforce the importance of designing written communication learning outcomes and providing faculty with support to teach and assess these learning outcomes, significant features that predate my role in faculty development. In effect, WPAs certainly have a seat at the table when reforming general education, especially when preserving the importance of first-year writing and designing learning outcomes around written communication.

GENERAL EDUCATION DESIGN TEAM: A PLACE
FOR WAC AND DIVERSITY AND INCLUSION

Once the essential learning outcomes were passed by the Faculty Senate in April 2016, the Faculty Senate appointed an Ad Hoc General Education Design Team. This team was charged primarily with recommending a model or models to implement the newly designed curriculum, as well as recommending a new name for general education. It was at this phase that the committee ran into some key obstacles of resistance; it was also at this phase that conversations and fears about resource allocation in relation to credit hour production emerged. Also at this phase, my work shifted from protecting first-year writing as a WPA to making the case for WAC programmatic resources combined with faculty development support.

Finally, it was at this phase that I began my role as associate director in OFD. When interviewing for the position, I emphasized an interest in developing WAC programming through our institution's teaching and learning center to support instructors teaching writing across disciplines. Previously in this chapter, I pointed to research that demonstrates one of WAC programs' purposes for helping students write appropriately in their chosen majors and fields of study; such scholarship also points to the need for WAC to pay more attention to the ways in which it might contribute to general education. While faculty in rhetoric and writing studies at WMU had previously made concerted efforts to make the case for written communication pedagogy across disciplines, while WPA specialists and program evaluators reported needs for stronger WAC components, and while there had been on-and-off-again efforts to study the impact of WAC on writing programs on WMU's campus, there were no formal plans to develop a WAC program. Based on my institutional memory, the designing of a new general education curriculum was the first time that faculty across fields began using the precise language "we need a WAC program." Thus, I saw my role in faculty development as an opportunity to make the case for WAC through the curricular model that the Design Team would develop.

Much of my focus shifted to ways that faculty development could contribute to the design, because the committee readily agreed that foundational courses in oral and written communication needed to be included as part of this plan. We also concurred that a course in quantitative literacy was essential. Where the committee struggled was on how to design courses that also included information literacy, digital communication, scientific literacy, and critical thinking. If the learning outcomes included these areas for enhancing intellectual and practical skills (see the previous discussion of the essential learning outcomes; WMU Faculty Senate 2016), how might a design reflect all of the skills students needed while keeping courses and credit hours reasonable so students could progress timely through their degree programs? Put simply, we learned relatively quickly that we could not design a required course for every single skill identified in the learning outcomes; some courses would have to emphasize more than one skill, whether it was covered across courses or within a single course.

As a committee, we agreed that certain classes, like oral communication, written communication, and quantitative literacy, would require their own courses, as such courses are consistent with the requirements offered across higher education general education programs. But we also needed to consider the fact that our program is not simply a reshuffling of current general education curricula; otherwise, there would be no need to revise or recreate a new model. As a result, we also referenced the Ad Hoc Committee on General Education's recommendations to build foundations, apply skills to content areas, and culminate a capstone experience for the program. Thus, we knew that not only would we have to make hard decisions about which classes required their own courses and which skills could be emphasized across courses, but we also had to determine at which levels, develop foundational skills and knowledge courses, and identify in which areas to apply skills to the content area courses, all while keeping credit hours within the ballpark of the current credit hour requirement in the general education program (33–36 credit hours) so students' progress toward degree completion would not be not delayed.

Table 2.1 reflects the design of our general education model for our program, WMU Essential Studies. It leads with the WMU Essential Studies Learning Outcomes (WMU Faculty Senate 2016). It requires students to first take a sequence of four foundational skills-based courses, at the foundations level; these courses include Writing, Communications (oral), Quantitative Literacy, and Inquiry and Engagement: Critical Thinking in the Humanities. The committee agreed that these skills require distinct courses and wanted to make sure students did not graduate without taking a humanities seminar. Sensitive of progress toward degree completion, we recognized that we could include no more than

Table 2.1. WMU Essential Studies model (WMU Faculty Senate 2018a)

Level 3: Connections					
Local and National Perspectives			Global Perspectives		

Level 2: Exploration and Discovery					
Personal Wellness	World Language and Culture	Science and Technology	Scientific Literacy with a Lab	Artistic Theory and Practice	Societies and Cultures

Level 1: Foundations			
Writing	Oral and Digital Communication	Quantitative Literacy	Inquiry and Engagement in the Humanities

four foundations classes for students to take, as students would need to take these classes as prerequisites for others in the sequence, preferably within the first year or two of study. We also recognized that some of the learning outcomes under the bullet "Enhance intellectual and practical skills" could not be captured by adding additional courses. Thus, while the committee agreed it was essential to have courses in first-year writing, oral communications, and quantitative literacy, skills such as applying information literacy and critical thinking (additional foundational skills) would need to be emphasized and connected with the other foundations courses. For instance, we sought to require information literacy as an outcome to be covered in Writing and Oral Communications foundations courses (see WMU Faculty Senate 2018a). With regard to critical thinking, we added that this outcome would be covered in the Inquiry and Engagement: Critical Thinking in the Arts and Humanities course. Thus, these four courses complete the foundations level, addressing the outcome, "enhancing intellectual and practical skills." The design also asks that instructors designate at least one assignment that speaks to either planetary sustainability or diversity and inclusion.

For the second level, Exploration and Discovery, six required courses address the following outcomes:

- Expand their understanding of human cultures and the physical/natural world;
- Exercise personal and social responsibility; and
- Exhibit integrative and applied learning.

These courses, Personal Wellness, World Language and Culture, Science and Technology, Laboratory Science, Artistic Theory and Practice, and Societies and Cultures, are also designed to replace the distribution requirements typically associated with general education curricula. While these courses bear similarity to most general education distribution categories, our model positions them in relation to essential learning outcomes, ones that build on a set of foundational skills. As previously stated in this chapter, the new model of WMU Essential Studies applies skills to content areas, as opposed to viewing course content categories in isolation. The Design Team was also cognizant of the need to revise general education so that students aren't simply approaching distribution areas as a menu or checklist of courses that have no clear connection with each other (WMU Faculty Senate 2018a, 3). In short, the explorations level comprises the bulk of the content-based courses. The Societies and Cultures course, a social science–based course, is writing-intensive, building from critical thinking and writing skills introduced at the foundations level. Both the Writing and Inquiry course and the Engagement: Critical Thinking in the Humanities course are prerequisites for the Societies and Cultures course. The courses in this section also address and are designed to assess the following WMU Essential Studies outcomes, previously passed by the Faculty Senate (see Faculty Senate 2018a):

- Demonstrate understandings and practices of personal wellness.
- Demonstrate familiarity with a language other than English and/or the culture associated with it.
- Demonstrate and apply scientific literacy.
- Increase knowledge of the arts.

Because the findings of the Ad Hoc Committee on General Education's self-study report indicated the need to develop a capstone experience that connected general education with a student's major (4), the Design Team included Level 3: Connections to accomplish this purpose. The committee decided against a specific capstone course for the program: first, because of sensitivity to students making timely progress toward degree completion, and second, because such a course might potentially compete with capstone courses offered in various departments and majors. Also of note, both courses are also either writing- or oral communication–intensive or both. Thus, the Writing course, the Inquiry and Engagement: Critical Thinking in the Humanities course, and Societies and Cultures course are each prerequisites for the two courses taken at this level. The two courses include Local and National Perspectives and Global Perspectives. Both courses should build upon the content introduced at the discoveries level, while also devoting care to the practice of diversity and inclusion, another learning outcome that is required for assessment at Level 3: Connections. While some faculty raised concerns about creating a false dichotomy that separates national and global perspectives, the committee agreed to create these as two distinct courses to make sure that students weren't simply engaging diversity and inclusion, and societies and cultures from a US historical and cultural context. To fulfill WMU's mission of global engagement, the committee agreed that a course that focused exclusively on global perspectives is necessary. Because the Level 3: Connections courses, both Global Perspectives and National Perspectives, reflect the capstone of the WMU Essential Studies program, three levels of learning outcomes are required: These include:

Student Primary Learning Outcome (Required):
- Apply ethical, critical, and informed thought within and across disciplines.

Student Secondary Learning Outcome (Select one):
- Apply different methods of intellectual inquiry, investigation, and discovery.
- Work both independently and in collaboration with others to achieve goals.
- Develop sensitivity to diversity and inclusion.
- Develop practices for planetary sustainability.

Student Foundational Learning Outcome (Select one):
- Demonstrate effective and appropriate written communication abilities.
- Demonstrate effective and appropriate oral and digital communication abilities. (Faculty Senate, WMU)

It is important to also emphasize the relationships between diversity and inclusion and writing-intensive courses. Pairing these two skills and outcomes together in the model greatly underscores the need for faculty development with emphasis on diversity and inclusion as well as oral and written communication competencies, all as essential twenty-first-century skills. General education reform has provided WMU with one of many opportunities to establish and develop collaborations between WAC and faculty development on creating diversity and inclusion programming (chapter 3 describes additional institutional opportunities).

WMU Essential Studies design, taken as a whole, places a strong emphasis on writing, oral communication, and critical thinking. The inclusion of five writing-intensive, oral communication, and critical thinking courses prompted additional conversations about how to train faculty to begin teaching writing and critical thinking, especially since many faculty tended to prioritize course content. During the design phase, faculty questioned both who should possess ownership over teaching critical thinking as a foundational skill, as well as concerns about how faculty would all of a sudden teach writing, given the fact that existing content-based courses had larger course caps than courses typically designated as writing-intensive; interestingly, conversations about ownership over oral communication skills were not debated, though WMU's school of communication expressed openness to oral communication skills being assessed in performing arts courses. Thus, the Design Team agreed to do focus groups with faculty with expertise in WAC or the teaching of writing, with me leading this group. The group was given the tasks of identifying logistical matters posed by the design and making recommendations that would need to be considered in order to move the WMU Essential Studies model forward. The WAC Focus Group recommended the following:

- WAC Program and Director
- Workshops with incentives for faculty to attend (stipends, reassigned course time, teaching endorsements etc.)
- Input in the course approval processes for writing-intensive courses
- A consortium of web-based resources for faculty teaching writing-intensive courses
- Input on University-Wide assessment of writing

These recommendations were presented to the Design Team and then forwarded to the Ad Hoc Logistics Team to be considered with the next phase of general education reform and implementation. The WAC Focus Group for the General Education Design Team, nonetheless, played an integral part in creating WAC on a campus that had never developed a university WAC program. WAC would thereafter serve as a point of continued conversation for implementation and logistics. The role of faculty development would also become intimately connected to the outreach, professional development, and resources needed to implement WMU Essential Studies successfully.

GENERAL EDUCATION LOGISTICS PLANNING: A PLACE FOR WAC AND FACULTY DEVELOPMENT

As previously discussed in this chapter, one primary rationale for general education reform was in response to HLC's findings that WMU does not sufficiently assess its general education program. Thus, as part of the Ad Hoc Logistics planning, the committee organized a Learning Outcomes

Rubric Event, where faculty would develop rubrics of varying levels of proficiency to align with the WMU Essential Studies Learning Outcomes Rubrics (see https://wmich.edu/facultysenate/wmuessentialstudies/wes rubrics). For the learning outcome "demonstrate effective oral, written, and digital communication abilities," groups of faculty volunteered to compose rubrics for oral and digital communication and written communication, and these rubrics would be used for assessment, first at Level 1: Foundations and then again with the Level 2: Societies and Cultures courses and Level 3: Connections courses, each of which build on Level 1 outcomes, usually those reflecting oralor digital communication, written communication, critical thinking, and information literacy outcomes. Most courses proposed at this level have been designed as writing-intensive, however. While digital communication does also happen in writing courses, it was agreed that the learning outcome would be assessed in oral communications classes, where those pedagogies have already been implemented by faculty within WMU's specific institutional context. Moreover, because Level 1: Foundations requires separate oral communications and writing courses, it was decided that two separate rubrics would be developed. Since oral and digital communication skills were being assessed in oral communication courses, the committee agreed that information literacy would be the other skill assessed in foundations writing courses, though information literacy does include a separate skill since courses at Levels 2 and 3 may select additional foundational skills besides writing to assess in those courses that are not writing-intensive.

The Learning Outcomes Rubric Event was perhaps one of the highlights of the committee's work, because it provided faculty with opportunities across disciplines to work collaboratively to determine what proficiency looks like within a particular skill or content area. It was also interesting to see that faculty who volunteered to work collaboratively on the written communication rubric were those who had not previously served on the WAC focus group. As leader of this group, while I was unsure how the committee would reach consensus on writing proficiency, I was pleasantly surprised to find much consistency and agreement across areas.

To begin the work of developing rubrics, the committee tasked each group with identifying two to three criteria that would be assessed, followed by descriptions of levels of proficiency (exemplary, proficient, developing, and beginning). We were also provided with sample rubrics, including the Association of American Colleges and Universities (AAC&U) Written Communication Value Rubric (see https://www

.aacu.org/value/rubrics/written-communication), as starting points to developing criteria. As a committee, we agreed this rubric would serve as a good starting point for developing our own; however, we were also strongly encouraged to narrow our criteria down to two or three in order to make assessment manageable for faculty teaching multiple sections. While we conceded to narrowing down criteria, as a committee we were uncomfortable with the task of only identifying two or three features of writing to assess written proficiency. Thus, we settled on four criteria and combined language and conventions together as one way to narrow down criteria from the Written Communication Value Rubric. We also questioned the clarity and meaning of the descriptions that align with the Value Rubric's proficiency areas, so we used the Value Rubric as a starting point to draft our own descriptions for proficiency levels. Table 2.2 reflects our final draft of the Foundations Writing Rubric after revisions and recommendations were provided and approved by the Ad Hoc Logistic subcommittee of assessment experts and specialists.

After feedback and revisions were implemented by the various faculty working groups on the outcomes rubrics, the logistics committee began discussing the need for providing professional development and support for faculty using these rubrics. The Logistics Committee then began working collaboratively with the WMU Technology Resources Center's instructional designers to provide course management technologies to display the rubrics and allow users to click the varying levels of proficiency as they correspond with the rubric criteria for each student; instructors would then submit their assessments through eLearning. Based on these plans, it became clear that additional resources and professional development would need to be offered for faculty on how to use the instructional technologies to do the assessment, how to design appropriate assignments or exams to align with the rubrics for assessment, and how to take students' examples to pilot the assessments. Thus, additional support and training with collaboration from faculty development and a writing assessment specialist with WAC experience would clearly be needed to assist faculty.

Once the Ad Hoc Design Team's model for the WMU Essential Studies curriculum was approved, the Faculty Senate appointed an Ad Hoc Logistics Committee to identify the key logistics matters that would need to be addressed concerning the implementation of WMU Essential Studies. This team was composed of administrators, faculty, academic advisors, and a representative from the Office of the Registrar, one who was charged with overseeing the publication of the course catalog. When the group first began meeting, they identified subcommittees to handle

Table 2.2. Level 1: Foundations Writing Rubric
Learning outcome: demonstrate effective and appropriate written communication abilities

Criteria	Exemplary	Proficient	Developing	Novice
CONTEXT AND PURPOSE FOR WRITING Student skillfully devotes careful attention to and consideration of audience, context, and purpose.	Devotes thorough and careful attention to audience, context, and purpose in the work; Approaches audience, purpose, and context with exceptional care and sophistication.	Devotes careful attention to context, audience, and purpose in most of the written work; devotes careful consideration to audience, context, and purpose.	Devotes some attention to context, audience, and purpose; lacks careful consideration and awareness of audience, context, and purpose in most of the work.	Devotes minimal attention to context, audience, and purpose; lacks consideration of audience, purpose, and context.
CONTENT DEVELOPMENT Student skillfully develops content appropriate to the subject or area of study.	Uses appropriate, relevant, and compelling content to illustrate mastery of the subject, conveying the writer's understanding and shaping the whole work.	Uses appropriate, relevant, and compelling content to explore ideas within the context of the discipline in most of the work.	Uses appropriate and relevant content to develop and explore ideas in some parts of the work.	Begins to use appropriate and relevant content to develop foundational ideas.
SOURCES AND EVIDENCE Student skillfully employs quality sources as evidence to support argument.	Employs high quality, credible, relevant sources as evidence appropriate for the discipline and genre of the writing.	Employs credible, relevant sources as evidence within the discipline and genre of the writing.	Attempts to employ credible and/or relevant sources as evidence appropriate for the discipline and genre of the writing, though sources are integrated inappropriately/incorrectly in some parts of the work.	Attempts to employ sources as evidence in the genre of writing, though sources may be integrated inappropriately/incorrectly.
LANGUAGE AND CONVENTIONS Student skillfully applies appropriate writing standards and conventions.	Produces correct spelling, grammar, syntax, word usage, and punctuation; successfully employs conventions particular to a specific discipline, including organization, content, presentation, formatting, and stylistic choices.	Produces few errors in spelling, grammar, word usage, and punctuation; employs most conventions particular to a specific discipline, including organization, content, presentation, and stylistic choices.	Produces some errors in spelling, grammar, syntax, word usage, punctuation, formatting, and citation; follows some expectations appropriate to a specific discipline for organization, content, and presentation.	Produces errors in spelling, grammar, syntax, word usage, punctuation, formatting, and citation that detract from the writing's meaning; attempts to use a consistent system for organization and presentation.

key logistic concerns. These included a subcommittee on transfer and accreditation, who was tasked with identifying logistics and challenges to implementation as they pertain to course transfer equivalencies from other institutions and high-credit-hour academic programs, and a marketing and communications subcommittee, whose task was to design a plan for preparing marketing and communication materials to advertise WMU Essential Studies. The Logistics Committee also kept record of the recommendations made from the previous WAC Focus Group.

While it was understood that not all of these recommendations could be implemented immediately, the Ad Hoc Logistics Committee was able to recommend that a budget protocol be submitted for a 50 percent (half-time) WAC coordinator to the administration. As part of the budget protocol's proposal, it was recommended that the WAC coordinator would organize efforts across campus to improve student writing, work with the Faculty Senate on course approvals of new and existing writing-intensive courses offered in WMU Essential Studies, and develop training and workshops for faculty teaching writing-intensive courses in WMU Essential Studies courses. It was also recommended that the WAC coordinator would report to the Office of Faculty Development (OFD). It was decided that the WAC coordinator would report to OFD because it already administers all of the workshops offered across campus, which would allow for stronger communication and coordination between the two units when designing and scheduling workshops, so they do not compete or conflict with each other. Positioning WAC under the broader umbrella of a teaching and learning center further reinforces the theory that professional development on writing instruction should aim to emphasize improved teaching, as opposed to improved student writing (Sandler 2000, 38).

It is also important to note that the WAC coordinator was one of two positions recommended by the budget protocol, with the other being a full-time director of WMU Essential Studies, who would not only work collaboratively with the WAC coordinator but would also coordinate the marketing and communication of the WMU Essential Studies program, coordinate with enrollment management, communicate and work collaboratively with local community colleges and feeder institutions on alignment between their general education programs and WMU Essential Studies, and coordinate assessment practices for measuring student learning outcomes in WMU Essential Studies courses. Prior to submitting the budget protocol, the Faculty Senate and senior-level administrators discussed whether or not the WAC coordinator would report to the director of WMU Essential Studies or to OFD. Eventually,

OFD was decided as the appropriate location for WAC professional development and outreach, because as a group the committee wanted to send the message that while writing plays a role in general education course designs, it is also important to provide professional development for faculty teaching writing-intensive courses in majors and professional programs. While general education reform served as the catalyst for WMU thinking more structurally as an institution about the importance of writing instruction, it is important to understand that writing instruction is also essential for teaching writing in the major or within the disciplines. Moreover, the fact that the baccalaureate writing requirement, where all students must take an upper-level writing course in their majors, is included as a separate requirement from the WMU Essential Studies curriculum, further emphasizes the need for WAC outreach beyond general education. In the end, the administration funded a half-time position for a WMU Essential Studies director, and a part-time faculty fellow for WAC, who would report to OFD. The faculty fellow hired was a rhetoric and composition scholar.

WMU ESSENTIAL STUDIES EXECUTIVE ADVISORY COMMITTEE: ASSESSING WRITING AND DIVERSITY AND INCLUSION OUTCOMES

I also served as an administrative representative for the WMU Essential Studies Executive Committee, seated by the Faculty Senate to oversee the implementation of the WES program that launched in fall 2020. The WES Executive Advisory Committee also includes the approved position of the WES director, one of two positions funded from the previous budget protocol from the provost's office. The absence of a WAC director required more collaboration with OFD, particularly with developing workshops to prepare faculty to design and submit courses for WES approval. The WES director has also sought to create faculty development initiatives around Writing to Learn, starting with OFD, since it had already developed a series of Writing to Learn workshops and was already in the process of creating a WAC learning community even before the WES design was implemented and approved. It is also critical to emphasize that many of OFD's efforts around providing workshops and web-based resources for writing instruction. In particular, its development of Writing to Learn workshops were created prior to my own tenure as associate director. OFD had also previously developed weekly writing retreats to support faculty over a period of several years prior to my arrival. Much of this programming reflects OFD's most recent Needs Assessment, where 85 percent of respondents requested more professional development on incorporating writing and communication skills in the classroom (WMOFD 2015, 8). Given that faculty were already familiar with OFD offerings and services as they pertained to the teaching of writing, incorporating a writing specialist to work more formally with OFD would be considered ideal.

In collaboration with OFD, the WES director, chair, and vice chair developed a series of workshops, "Navigating WMU Essential Studies: Design, Assess, Submit." These workshops include "three concurrent breakout sessions":

Breakout A, Understanding the WMU Essential Studies Design: Where Does My Course Fit? What Is Needed for a Successful Review

Breakout B, Assessing WMU Essential Studies Student Learning Outcomes: What Assessment Evidence Is Needed

Breakout C, Electronic Submission Process (https://wmich.edu/ facultysenate/wmuessentialstudies)

Issues for WAC and diversity and inclusion work were very apparent in Breakout B, with its focus on learning outcomes and assessment. To submit a course for WES approval, faculty or department units must complete an electronic curriculum proposal that also includes a syllabus identifying which learning outcomes will be assessed (some required, some optional) and an assessment plan that states both what assessment activities will be included in alignment with the student learning outcomes and when the assessment will take place. To assist faculty with developing assessment plans, the WES program also created a new website, with an interactive tutorial for assessing learning outcomes (see https:// wmich.edu/facultysenate/wmuessentialstudies/wmuessentialstudies -interactivetutorials).

When instructors select a course category within the interactive tutorial, the link leads them to the outcome rubrics developed for each category. For those courses that require written communication, instructors are able to view the written proficiency rubric, which was developed and approved by faculty. At first, questions arose about how detailed faculty assessment plans needed to be. In other words, faculty wanted to know if they needed to attach copies of their writing assignments or topics. The WES Executive Advisory Committee simply concluded that a description of the writing assignment and when the assessment would take place would suffice for initial review. Additional questions about resourcing writing classes were also addressed at the Navigating Western Essential Studies workshops. For example, courses in both Level 2: Societies and

Table 2.3. Diversity and Inclusion Outcomes Rubric

Criteria	Exemplary	Proficient	Developing	Beginning
DEVELOP AWARENESS Demonstrate awareness of how diversity and inclusion affect yourself and others.	Engage in meaningful interactions that promote diversity and inclusion.	Explain how differences in perspectives affect issues of diversity and inclusion.	Describe perspectives on diversity and inclusion that differ from your own.	Identify your own perspectives on diversity and inclusion.
HISTORICAL PERSPECTIVE Demonstrate awareness of how diversity and inclusion have been affected by continuities and changes over time	Engage in meaningful interactions that promote commitment to diversity and inclusion.	Explain how continuities and changes over time have affected diversity and inclusion.	Describe the continuities and changes over time that have affected diversity and inclusion.	Identify continuities and changes over time that have affected diversity and inclusion.

Cultures and Level 3: Connections now include a written communication learning outcome, while the previous general education categories that most closely match the content for these WES courses did not include writing-intensive courses. Moreover, previous Memorandums of Action passed by the Faculty Senate also specify twenty-five to thirty students as the ideal course size for all Level 3: Connections courses, while course caps for many of these courses still enrolled one hundred or more students. As such, faculty attending these workshops raised questions about how to assess writing using the outcomes rubrics in large-size classes. The view of the WES director and Executive Advisory Committee is that smaller class sizes are necessary to assess writing effectively, and the workshops developed in collaborations between OFD and WES have elevated the conversation about the necessity of WAC support and training, bringing it to the attention of senior-level administration.

The creation of WES also provided the institution with opportunities to develop diversity and inclusion learning outcomes that could be assessed across area categories, including writing-intensive courses. Table 2.3 identifies the diversity and inclusion learning outcomes students would be expected to demonstrate as part of the WES program; these criteria include developmental awareness and historical perspectives.

As part of the Navigating Western Essential Studies workshops, many faculty asked for clarification of the diversity and inclusion requirements, since they were part of the WES program despite no single course mandating them. At Level 1: Foundations, instructors are required to include at least one assignment designed around either planetary sustainability or diversity and inclusion. Instructors are then provided with the option of selecting diversity and inclusion as one of two learning outcomes for Level 2 and one of three learning outcomes for Level 3. Discussion about specific assessment activities that could effectively measure developing sensitivity to diversity and inclusion naturally emerged around writing assignments and Writing to Learn activities, though it was acknowledged that exams, group projects, and other assignment activities could also be used to assess the diversity and inclusion outcomes. To continue professional development around both WES and diversity and inclusion, OFD then expanded its workshops for new and returning faculty by adding new workshops, including An Overview of WMU Essential Studies, and Diversity and Inclusion in the Classroom, in addition to previous WAC and diversity and inclusion programming offered by OFD, as will be described in the next chapter. In addition to these workshops, OFD has also added additional workshops on information literacy, a learning outcome that is required for Level 1: Foundations writing courses; in doing so, it also expanded some of its writing-intensive programming. Thus, conversations about general education reform led to an increase in professional development on both WAC and diversity and inclusion.

INITIAL ASSESSMENT DATA FROM WES

After the first year of launching WES, instructors were asked to submit data and responses to the outcomes for Writing, Oral and Digital Communication, Societies and Cultures, and World Languages and Cultures. Other outcomes would be reviewed in subsequent years. The Diversity and Inclusion and Sustainability outcomes are reviewed annually along with the other outcomes. For year one, the following data were collected with respect to the Writing and Diversity and Inclusion learning outcomes:

What is interesting from the initial round of data is how similar the scores are for both writing and diversity and inclusion, with the average score being proficient in all categories. Surprisingly, though, the average scores on Language and Conventions and Context and Purpose for Writing tied for highest across each category for writing (table 2.4), though in the workshops I did for teaching about SRTOL (students' right to their own language) and language awareness (see chapter 5), instructors often made the most complaints about students' poor writing skills, specifically in the area of Language and Conventions. Also noteworthy, though perhaps not as surprising, is students' greater proficiency in the Developing Awareness category toward diversity and inclusion

Table 2.4. 2020 WMU Essential Studies Results Summary: Demonstrate effective and appropriate communication skills

	Total Students Evaluated	*Total Sections Evaluated*	*Average Score*	*4: Exemplary*	*3: Proficient*	*2: Developing*	*1: Beginning*
Context and Purpose for Writing	1,512	77	3.13	0.37	0.45	0.14	0.05
Content Development	1,549	77	3.12	0.38	0.42	0.15	0.06
Sources and Evidence	1,493	77	3.00	0.34	0.41	0.17	0.08
Language and Conventions	1,530	77	3.13	0.38	0.43	0.13	0.06

Table 2.5. Fall 2020 WMU Essential Studies Results Summary: Develop sensitivity to diversity and inclusion

	Total Students Evaluated	*Total Sections Evaluated*	*Average Score*	*4: Exemplary*	*3: Proficient*	*2: Developing*	*1: Beginning*
Develop Awareness	982	37	3.14	0.35	0.48	0.12	0.05
Historical Perspectives	980	37	3.09	0.36	0.44	0.15	0.06

in comparison to the category of Historical Perspective (table 2.5). According to these data, however, faculty development programming could benefit learning by helping students understand the connections between sources and uses of evidence (Sources and Evidence category, table 2.4), which scored the lowest among the writing categories, and understanding historical perspectives (Historical Perspective category, table 2.5), which also scored the lowest among the diversity and inclusion categories. Connecting students' ability to incorporate sources as evidence can also assist students with using the appropriate evidence needed to understand how history impacts how we understand diversity and inclusion, especially during a time when the uses, or nonuses, of anti-racist scholarship are being attacked by legislature, school boards, and parents.

In order to gain better understanding of the relationships between sources and historical perspectives, it is also important to look at preliminary data reported for the information literacy learning outcome below:

Of the three categories of learning outcomes analyzed in this chapter, students scored the least proficient with regard to information literacy.

Table 2.6. Fall 2020 WMU Essential Studies Results Summary: Demonstrate and apply information literacy

	Total Students Evaluated	Total Sections Evaluated	Average Score	4: Exemplary	3: Proficient	2: Developing	1: Beginning
Students Are Consumers of Information	1,463	63	3.03	0.41	0.27	0.27	0.05
Students Are Creators of Information	1,462	63	2.80	0.37	0.28	0.14	0.21

While students are more proficient at consuming information, whether factual or not, they are least proficient at creating information. Also crucial is understanding the connections between the processes used to consume information and the processes for creating information. While students evaluated in each of these categories overlap, a more in-depth look at evidence and citation practices can help us understand how students use evidence to create information and make meaning within their own historical contexts and beyond.

Additional assessment data also suggest looking at creative and critical thinking; demonstrating familiarity with a language other than English or with the culture associated with it; applying ethical, critical, and informed thought across the disciplines, as each set of skills and knowledge area shapes how we understand diversity and inclusion as well as writing. Tables 2.7, 2.8, and 2.9 provide results for both sets of learning outcomes:

In most cases, the data demonstrate proficiency, with a few exceptions I will highlight. While the scores for "demonstrating familiarity with a language other than English and/or the culture associated with it" indicates proficiency similar to those for written communication and diversity and inclusion, the rubric criteria that emphasize critical thinking skills, including Critical Thinking ("develop creative and critical thinking") and Critical Thought ("apply ethical, critical, and informed thought within or across disciplines"), are two of the three that score below 3.00—that is, proficient. Similarly, creative thinking scores below 3.00. It is especially important to highlight these areas, as my discussion is informed by the CWPA Framework for Success in Postsecondary Writing. In particular, creativity ("the ability to use novel approaches for generating, investigating, an representing ideas"), responsibility ("the ability to take ownership of one's actions and understand the consequences of those actions for oneself and others"), and metacognition ("the ability to reflect on one's own thinking as well as on the individual

Table 2.7. Fall 2020 WMU Essential Studies Results Summary: Develop creative and critical thinking

	Total Students Evaluated	Total Sections Evaluated	Average Score	4: Exemplary	3: Proficient	2: Developing	1: Beginning
Creative Thinking	1,410	54	2.80	0.29	0.37	0.20	0.14
Critical Thinking	3,173	103	2.89	0.34	0.33	0.22	0.12
Creative and Critical Habits of Mind	3,382	107	2.85	0.34	0.31	0.21	0.14

Table 2.8. Fall 2020 WMU Essential Studies Results Summary: Demonstrate familiarity with a language other than English and/or the culture associated with it

	Total Students Evaluated	Total Sections Evaluated	Average Score	4: Exemplary	3: Proficient	2: Developing	1: Beginning
Communication	223	17	3.01	0.30	0.45	0.22	0.03
Cultural Knowledge	434	23	3.14	0.38	0.41	0.18	0.03
Cultural Comparisons	476	25	3.12	0.34	0.45	0.17	0.03

Table 2.9. Fall 2020 WMU Essential Studies Results Summary: Apply ethical, critical, and informed thought within or across disciplines

	Total Students Evaluated	Total Sections Evaluated	Average Score	4: Exemplary	3: Proficient	2: Developing	1: Beginning
Ethical Thought	296	17	3.02	0.33	0.41	0.21	0.05
Critical Thought	296	18	2.98	0.34	0.34	0.34	0.34
Thinking within One Discipline	203	15	3.09	0.38	0.37	0.20	0.04
Thinking across Disciplines	195	12	3.02	0.39	0.31	0.22	0.08

and cultural processes used to structure knowledge") each connect to the "habits of mind" that determine how students understand, communicate, and share knowledge across academic disciplines ("Framework" 2011). In essence, while each of these rubrics were developed by separate groups of faculty, the connections between how we understand skills and knowledge using writing and diversity and inclusion content are key to students' successes in general education.

Based on this initial look at the assessment data, it is clear that the rubrics are works in process and imprecise to some degree. For example, neither the rubrics for writing nor those for information literacy address precisely how students locate, evaluate, and integrate sources and information. That said, based on this initial assessment it is clear that a cultural shift around professional development and faculty development has at least in part influenced how curriculum is approached at WMU. Prior to the launch of WES, there was no formal, programmatic sharing of best practices, no culture of formal reflection on pedagogical practices, no University-wide reflection on programmatic assessment beyond the institution's Assessment in Action Day, which allows faculty to share individual programmatic assessment initiatives. Now, there is a culture of collecting, analyzing, and discussing assessment data around general education.

CONCLUSION

The implementation of the WES program to revise its previous general education program provided WMU as an institution with an opportunity to prioritize writing instruction and diversity and inclusion across campus through more formal structures and partnerships. Two of the key pieces to providing faculty with the resources and support needed to revise and create new general education courses have been (1) professional development through existing campus teaching and learning centers and (2) WAC programmatic outreach. At WMU, though not a formalized structure, collaborative efforts between faculty development and general education programs can provide training and workshops, while also using assessment of writing and diversity and inclusion outcomes to make recommendations on assessment practices and course approval processes. While currently WAC is not a stand-alone unit with its own budget and administrative support, I believe that increasing developments with WAC-based activities have been consistent with the advice offered by Sandler about starting WAC on a college campus. While I've initiated an active role in leading WAC focus groups and initiatives on campus, I've never attempted to start a WAC program on my own (Sandler 2000, 37)—in fact, I pitched the need for a WAC program, but the budget protocol advocating a WAC coordinator was not proposed by me at all; later, after leaving OFD, I was able to advocate for a WAC faculty fellow in the absence of a formal program. The challenge, however, remains for scholars and administrators of color doing diversity and inclusion advocacy. Unfortunately, when representing the groups and constitutions from which we share a collective identity and set of experiences, on many occasions our work continues to be perceived as self-serving.

When designing WAC and diversity and inclusion initiatives, I have also really tried to organize as many teachers across campus interested in writing as possible, even though most of these teachers did not have formal training in writing pedagogy, and I've relied minimally on my home English department to lead WAC initiatives. Perhaps my work through OFD has provided me with more opportunity to work across campus, as opposed to relying only on rhetoric and writing studies faculty in English. Finally, with the Writing to Learn, Writing Across the Curriculum, and Teaching Inclusivity workshops I previously facilitated through OFD, I have worked hard to emphasize the importance of excellence in teaching over the improvement of student writing through inclusive practices. This emphasis, I believe, has gone a long way in building stronger relationships between teaching and learning and WAC initiatives on campus (Sandler 2000, 37–38).

In effect, general education reform is a large task upon which to embark for any institution; it is a task that takes a lot of time and commitment, institutionally and from each of its stakeholders. WAC programs and faculty development centers are key stakeholders who deserve a seat at the table when identifying priorities and resources for general education reform. The ability for WAC and faculty development centers to work formally through stronger partnerships and collaborations further highlights the pressing needs, such as support services and resources for faculty, required to demonstrate teaching excellence in general education core curricula.

3

THE WORK OF WRITING NEVER ENDS
Writing Across the Curriculum and Diversity and Inclusion Professional Development Opportunities

Building on previous scholarship that connects faculty development with diversity and inclusion, I argue that rhetoric and composition has a history of missing opportunities to play active roles in campus-wide conversations surrounding diversity and inclusion, and that WAC programmatic development, a subfield that traditionally has not considered race (Anson 2012), may serve as a future bridge for such possibilities. In the last chapter of *Afrocentric Teacher-Research* (2013), I proposed that we forward the struggle for language rights by communicating to audiences outside of rhetoric and composition at our institutional sites. I further proposed using WAC outreach as a venue for aligning our work with the Language Across the Curriculum (LAC) movement in higher education and with institutional missions that promote diversity and inclusion. This chapter, then, responds to the call in chapter 6 of *Afrocentric Teacher-Research* to create additional opportunities to promote diversity, including linguistic diversity in WAC outreach.

As I've thought about how my own work responds to that call, I've also thought more about the ways in which WAC can contribute more broadly to diversity and inclusion outreach by collaborating with faculty development and teaching and learning centers. In some ways this response is more nuanced than those proposed in chapter 6 of *Afrocentric Teacher-Research.* While that call proposes WAC as a venue for outreach, its audience is still mostly directed at WPAs doing work in writing programs (114–15). What I've learned from my work in OFD, however, is that in order to effect larger-scale institutional change, we not only need to promote linguistic diversity outside and beyond university writing programs (119), but also, and more importantly, we have much to offer about teaching and learning topics as they relate to diversity and inclusion through rhetorical education and professional development. By the same token, teaching and learning centers offer writing teachers and WPAs opportunities to think about the extra-roles

https://doi.org/10.7330/9781646424542.c003

for professional development with respect to diversity and inclusion. As such, professional development workshops emphasizing diversity and inclusion provide writing teachers with additional opportunities to improve teaching practices that extend far beyond writing pedagogy. It is through these alliances that institutions might build stronger foundations of diversity training in higher education and writing pedagogy for instructors across disciplines.

Using my experience designing both WAC and diversity and inclusion programming on campus, this chapter describes the ways in which training and expertise in WAC and faculty development help administrators—in particular, college deans—craft large-scale leadership initiatives that assist with retention and student enrollment. Building on examples of programs created for WAC and faculty development, I describe the ways in which the work developed from these programs has shaped the work I do as an academic administrator. Experiences with WPA work, WAC, and faculty development leadership provide transferable skills that may potentially lead to administration.

In this chapter, I first review the different models used to form faculty development and WAC partnerships: both indirect, where informal collaborations are formed through faculty interests, and direct, where formal and designated institutional spaces and infrastructures are used to facilitate these partnerships. Next, I reflect on the diversity and inclusion initiatives I've developed through OFD, and the ways in which WAC contributes to and benefits from faculty development workshops that promote diversity and inclusion. Using reflections on my work with faculty development diversity and inclusion initiatives as a framework, this chapter identifies the ways in which WAC outreach and rhetorical approaches to teaching argument enhance teaching and learning professional development opportunities for all faculty. This chapter also specifically discusses OFD's Teaching Inclusivity summer seminar and workshop series. With these efforts, my aim is to make the case for the ways in which WAC outreach enhances teaching and learning, and what WAC specialists and leaders can learn about diversity and inclusion competencies in higher education. In doing so, I seek to show the ways in which formal alliances and partnerships might be reciprocal.

Finally, I draw upon WMU's University College model of establishing the Merze Tate College. The Merze Tate College is named after the first African American woman to graduate from WMU, who also received her PhD from Harvard. Its namesake and foci strengthen and enhance diversity. Specific components of the Merze Tate College include a centralized model that merges student and career success, academic advising, WMU Essential Studies (general education), and the Writing Center under one centralized college that focuses on diversity, equity, and student enrollment.

A REVIEW OF WAC AND FACULTY DEVELOPMENT PARTNERSHIPS

Significant scholarship in rhetoric and composition has identified direct and indirect connections between faculty development, teaching and learning centers, and WAC programs. While there are clear connections between the work that WAC directors, WPAs, and faculty developers do, as a WPA, faculty developer, and former associate dean, I am most interested in the rhetorical strategies that program administrators might employ to make these partnerships and collaborations more fruitful and responsive to twenty-first-century needs regarding campus climate in higher education. For the purposes of this book, I identify diversity and inclusion as one area that demands the attention of both WAC practitioners and faculty developers; however, it is also essential to understand the rhetorical tools necessary to do intellectual work around diversity and inclusion within systems of higher education.

Prior to identifying these strategies, it is first important to review the body of literature as it pertains to WAC and faculty development partnerships. In the first part of this chapter, I review scholarship that mentions brief connections between WAC programmatic work and faculty development centers. I identify these collaborations by their indirect connections, in that the sources explicitly do not claim that their purpose is to focus on collaborations between faculty development and WAC. Instead, these sources make brief references to WAC or faculty development as used to effect institutional development as it pertains exclusively to teaching and learning. In the next section of this chapter, I identify explicit and direct connections between faculty development and WAC. These direct connections identify specific partnerships and alliances for transforming teaching and learning environments on campus, often through writing pedagogy and professional development.

Before identifying indirect and direct connections between faculty development centers and WAC programs, it is also important to clarify the type of faculty development to which I refer when exploring potential for formal partnerships and collaborations. While faculty development as a practice is often part of the work that WPAs and WAC directors do when facilitating professional development workshops on the teaching of writing, for the purposes of this book I am interested in faculty development as a center, location, or programmatic structure for professional development that provides faculty and instructors with the resources and tools necessary to do work with special emphasis on teaching and learning activities. Put simply, I focus on faculty development as a location or structure exclusively devoted to professional development for faculty, not as the practice of professional development that one might offer from time to time outside of a specific center or designated role. Virginia S. Lee identifies five structures for educational or faculty development centers. They include the following:

1. Single, centralized teaching and learning center
2. Individual faculty member, within or without a physical center
3. A committee that supports faculty development
4. A clearinghouse for programs and offerings
5. Structures such as system-wide offices. (Sorcinelli, Austin, and Eddy 2006, 23)

As indicated from this list, there is a wide range of structures for faculty development work, but my interest in faculty development partnerships aligns most closely with "system-wide offices" (23), a structure that is most consistent with my institution's organizational structure. Moreover, given the abundance of scholarship that calls for the breaking of university silos to foster stronger collaboration across units (Kolowich 2010; Mandernach et al. 2014), I am interested in cross-campus units or offices for collaborations that enable faculty teaching across disciplines to engage beyond a particular department or academic unit. While collaborations can indeed occur with those appointed to a faculty development committee or with a specific faculty member designated to do the work of faculty development, those structures of work often resemble the model of service and committee work used at college and department levels, locations that often reinscribe academic silos. In contrast, a center or location that serves the entire university serves as a potential hub for collaboration across units. Intellectual work designed for faculty development, WAC, and diversity and inclusion provide fruitful opportunities to explore these collaborations.

The role of writing centers in relation to faculty development is also critical to understanding higher education partnerships. Writing centers have been well-used institutional resources to provide pedagogical workshops for both faculty and tutors. Linda S. Bergmann's (2008) "Writing Centers and Cross-Curricular Literacy Programs as Models for Faculty Development" provides a review of three critical works related to the subject, including: Jeffry Jablonsky's *Academic Writing Consulting and WAC: Methods and Models for Guiding Cross-curricular Literacy Work*, Geller and coauthors' *The Everyday Writing Center: A Community of Practice*, and Christina Murphy and Brian Stay's *The Writing Center Director's Resource Book*. Bergmann begins by writing:

> Faculty development often gets a bad reputation, sometimes for very good reasons. Faculty may be coerced to attend sessions at which they are required to listen to speakers on topics selected by administrators (and occasionally trustees), topics about which the faculty have little interest except to figure out the subtext, that is, what top-down "good idea" is going to be imposed on their teaching or research lives this time. Sometimes what is called faculty development involves applying business models to education, as in the Total Quality Management initiatives that many of us endured in the early nineties. (524)

Bergmann's review of these works is not absent a discussion of race and cultural and linguistic diversity, however. In her review of *The Everyday Writing Center*, Bergmann also writes the following:

> The Everyday writers discuss how, for example, tutor training books commonly set aside—or segregate—a chapter on race and cultural/linguistic diversity but seldom consider how ideas about race are interwoven with the daily practices and assumptions of writing instructors both in and outside the writing center—no matter how nice, sensitive, and unprejudiced members of the dominant race or cultural group may try to be. Using an adaptation of the inventory Peggy McIntosh developed in "White Privilege: Unpacking the Invisible Knapsack" (2005), they propose an inventory of attitudes that writing tutors (presumably mostly white) can use to understand their own privileged position in the academy and their practices in the writing center and to become conscious of the dominant (white) discourse valued by the academy no matter what the race of the writer. (530)

INDIRECT CONNECTIONS BETWEEN FACULTY DEVELOPMENT AND WAC CENTERS AND PROGRAMS

In the second edition of *A Guide to Faculty Development*, Gillespie and Robertson (2010) indicate that faculty development programs in US higher education were initially designed in the 1950s and 1960s to assist faculty members with becoming successful with regard to "disciplinary expertise and research" (4). In the 1960s and 1970s, faculty development programs shifted foci in ways that "intertwined with two concurrent important social movements: the human potential and the student rights movements" (5). As a result of these movements, faculty development programs began to shift more toward a focus on excellence in teaching (5). Interestingly enough, this shift to teaching excellences runs concurrent with the Conference on College Composition and Communication (CCCC)'s focus on student rights, with the 1974 adoption of the CCCC Students' Right to Their Own Language resolution. The resolution's intention was to respond to "how teachers instruct students whose heritage languages differ from the more hegemonic varieties traditionally endorsed by schools" (Perryman-Clark, Kirkland, and Jackson 2014, 1–2), therefore underscoring a focus on both teaching excellence and teaching students of historically oppressed groups, an intention that coincides with shifts in faculty development programs that accompanied the Open Admissions movements in higher education. That said, the work of faculty development programs and CCCC initiatives surrounding language rights has remained separate: the work of CCCC remained confined to the teaching of writing within the organization. This, however, is not a surprise, given the fact that SRTOL "became one of the most controversial position statements passed in the history of CCCC" (1), therefore suggesting that CCCC as an organization was not quite ready for broader outreach beyond the organization. Nonetheless, the fact that these movements remained separate indicates a missed opportunity for faculty development partnerships around student writing.

More explicitly, *A Guide to Faculty Development* makes a couple of references to writing programs in its discussion of professional development. Gillespie and Robertson assert:

> In addition to strong oral communication skills, effective writing communication skills are important to the educational developer in order to summarize pedagogical resource material for faculty members, write promotional material to promote workshops or institutes, draft instructional policies, construct letters of recommendation, and develop administrative reports. The ability to write to a variety of disciplines and different levels within the organization is a standard part of the job. (93)

In their discussion of writing, the ability to write effectively focuses mostly on the necessity for faculty developers to write for a wide range of audiences, as opposed to helping faculty develop the pedagogical tools necessary to teach writing across various disciplines, something that WAC programs are often called upon to do. In another section on professional development, Gillespie and Robertson discuss writing programs as necessary for helping graduate students, noting that "most programs address academic writing in some fashion via workshops or courses, . . . writing across the curriculum, grading, writing a dissertation or writing within the discipline" (332). While WAC is mentioned within this context, the context is restricted to a discussion on faculty development programs explicitly designed to help graduate students. Moreover, while WAC is mentioned as part of the work surrounding professional development for graduate students, the description of the relationship between faculty developers and WAC programs is a brief one that does not thoroughly address extensive partnerships and initiatives. Put simply, it is not clear to what extent faculty development centers and WAC programs might collaborate on initiatives surrounding the professional development of both graduate and undergraduate students.

Scholarship on WAC intellectual work has similarly nodded briefly to the role of faculty development in professionalizing teachers of writing. In *Writing Across the Curriculum: A Guide to Developing Programs*, Susan H. McLeod and Margot Soven (2000) argue that "faculty development is an essential part of writing across the curriculum—almost all programs at one time or another hold workshops for faculty to discuss WAC concepts and to demonstrate techniques of assigning and evaluating student writing" (5). She later concludes: "faculty development is an integral part of your WAC program, you will find that workshops become integral as well" (33). While faculty development is touched upon in several forms throughout her book, McLeod's emphasis is on faculty development as an intellectual practice or tool needed to create a successful program, as opposed to faculty development as a center or opportunity for formal partnerships and collaborations.

Other contributions in *Writing Across the Curriculum: A Guide to Developing Programs* draw similar parallels between the work of faculty developers and WAC programs. While both faculty development centers and WAC programs similarly use both workshop and institute models for professional development, Karen Wiley Sandler (2000) provides some practical advice as it pertains to the role of faculty development when creating a campus WAC program. Some of this advice includes collaborating on campus initiatives with a larger group (as opposed to starting a program by oneself), making connections across campus, finding teachers with reputations for teaching excellence, providing lead teachers with the support they need, and using workshops to improve teaching and not simply writing (38–39). Much of this advice parallels the missions of faculty development programs. In their survey of successful faculty development programs, Sorcinelli, Austin, and Eddy (2006) identify the following top three goals of successful faculty development programs:

- Creating or sustaining a culture of teaching excellence (72%)
- Responding to individual faculty members' needs (56%)
- Advancing new initiatives in teaching and learning (49%). (43)

While much of Sandler's advice for creating WAC programs is consistent with the mission of faculty development programs, again, this discussion does not identify WAC programs and faculty development centers as opportunities for direct collaborations or extensive programmatic initiatives; instead both programs are positioned as doing similar work in isolation of each other, thereby reinforcing academic silos in higher education.

While some scholarship makes clear connections between faculty development programs and WAC, other scholarship positions WAC as an example of faculty development done at specific universities. In other words, WAC is not a separate program itself, but one of many faculty development initiatives a campus might offer. While this might seem to connect the two on the surface, the relationships between how the two areas of intellectual work engage are not always explicit or direct. One example of this is a discussion of the University of Cincinnati's faculty development model, as discussed in the article "Rethinking Faculty Development." Lanthan D. Camblin Jr. and Joseph A. Steger identify the history of faculty development at their institutions, naming key initiatives that were created under the auspices of faculty development, noting:

> During the 1980s, the University expanded its menu of faculty development activities and initiated several specialized projects. These efforts included Writing Across the Curriculum, Learning Across the Curriculum, All-University Faculty Retreats, the Project Improve and Reward Teaching (PIRT), the University Research Council, the Center for Academic Instructional Technologies, and the Library Technology Assistance Group. Collectively, more than half of the total faculty and administrators have participated in and benefited from these efforts. (6)

It is important to note that the previous quotation includes the only mention of WAC featured in the entire article. As previously emphasized, the degree to which faculty development specialists and WAC faculty and specialists collaborated formally or engaged each other is not clear. What is clear from the article, though, is the history of moves from faculty development activities in the 1980s, to a faculty development committee in the 1990s, and now presently to a formal center for teaching and learning. When accessing the program offerings from the University of Cincinnati's Center for Teaching and Learning (CET&L) website, readers can view a list of program offerings and partners, none of which include WAC (see https://www.uc.edu/about/cetl.html). Thus, while WAC is clearly a part of the work that faculty developers do with regard to professional development, the ways in which these units work together remains less clear.

In their book, *Faculty Development in the Age of Evidence: Current Practices, Future Imperatives*, Andrea L. Beach and coauthors (2016) identify several approaches to faculty development. Specifically, in chapter

4, they provide a summary of signature approaches identified from a survey of faculty developers. These approaches include faculty learning communities (FLCs), discipline-specific programs, informal discussions with colleagues, institutes and retreats, web-based resources, seminars in a series, and structured discussions on readings (81–85). The only mention of writing programming offered, however, is an example of the University of Vermont's Writing in the Disciplines program, which they identify as a signature example of institutions and retreats (83). Clearly, such an example encompasses several of the principles identified by the authors as informing the area of faculty development; these range from a promotion of preparation and professional development, to enhancing diversity, to meeting institutional needs, to reflecting "institutional commitment, collaboration, and recognition . . . [as] community work" (7). However, with particular reference to the collaborations, a principle that the authors reference in multiple instances (7, 28, 35–38, 71, 100, 120–21, 134–35), WAC programming collaborations with faculty development and teaching and learning centers are not emphasized. In all fairness, this observation is not intended as criticism, especially given that the authors acknowledge the need to collaborate and meet institutional needs. What is most important to emphasize here is that there are ample opportunities for stronger collaborations between WAC programs and faculty development centers in ways that are more formal and direct than the relationships implied by Beach and colleagues' discussion.

As a rhetoric and composition scholar, I recognize that there may be legitimate reasons for keeping WAC and faculty development centers separate in their programming, particularly for those teachers and scholars devoted to the teaching and study of writing. I would certainly concede that for far too long, institutions of higher education have operated from the assumption that anyone can teach writing regardless of academic discipline. During the summer of 2017, readers of higher education and news editorials found varying degrees of opinion offered about the legitimacy of writing teachers and first-year writing, and scholars in rhetoric and writing have provided tremendous responses rebutting claims made by those outside of the field. Seth Kahn's (2016) commentary, "Bad Idea about Writing: Anybody Can Teach It," is perhaps one of the strongest rebuttals. In the following, Kahn characterizes the notion of "anybody" teaching writing:

> If you've never thought about specialized training for people who teach writing, that's no surprise—the idea itself hasn't been around for long. Because of its low level (101 is about the lowest number a credit-bearing college course could have) and its content (traditionally, low-level

grammar concerns, citation formats for research papers and similar remediations that most people think students should have learned in high school), it's not so surprising that decision makers would conclude that anybody can do it. (par. 5)

Kahn concludes by describing some of the credentialing of teacher-scholars of writing, including those who typically would have "graduate degrees (most already do, of course, often more than one), and . . . would have spent years on the job (many already have). Many (more) would have conducted research into effective teaching or other kinds of research that help them teach writing" (par. 12). His statements about credentialing are well supported by CCCC and and the Council of Writing Program Administrators (CWPA). CCCC's "Principles for the Postsecondary Teaching of Writing" explicitly states that instructors teaching writing should have backgrounds and experiences in theories of writing that include but are not limited to professional development, participation in disciplinary conferences, and coursework in rhetoric and composition (CCCC 2015; see "Principle 10").

Kahn's context in relation to first-year writing, however, is critical, because his argument is also situated in relation to the notion of "anyone" teaching writing as linked to cheap—often adjunct—labor, a labor market that disproportionately affects first-year writing programs. His notion of credentialing, though, does not seem to include those faculty who assign writing in courses outside of first-year composition—those who, though credentialed in the content areas associated with their disciplines, bear no responsibility in teaching writing. In fact, the CCCC "Principles for the Postsecondary Teaching of Writing" (2015) acknowledges the following:

> While first-year writing courses are critical for engaging students in the practice and study of writing, writing abilities will grow only with focused attention throughout a college career. All faculty bear responsibility and possess the ability to teach the writing and inquiry practices of their discipline. Helping writers recognize the heuristic value of the act of writing will demonstrate to them how powerful writing can be in facilitating and transferring what they learn. ("Principle 8")

This principle further reinforces the need for WAC programs and outreach. Identifying WAC as a disciplinary threshold concept, Linda Adler-Kassner and John Majewski assert that the "entire WAC movement is founded on the belief that all teachers of all subjects share responsibility for supporting the development of advanced student literacies" (2016, 209). Thus, while it is important to credential and name the work that we do in rhetoric and composition, work that qualifies us uniquely to lead WAC programs and initiatives, it does not mean that such work has to remain distinctly separated from the work of faculty developers and teaching and learning centers. What I argue later in this book, however, is that WAC work can be part of the work that we do in faculty development and teaching learning centers. These connections, instead, can be stronger: more collaborative, direct, and formal.

To be clear, proposing formal faculty development and WAC programmatic partnerships does not suggest that faculty development centers assume ownership of the WAC professional development, especially if those who lead and administer such centers do not have specific training in rhetoric and composition. Consistent with the CWPA Portland Resolution, which identifies WAC directors as examples of WPA roles on college campuses, WPA credentialing and qualifications include the following:

- teaching composition and rhetoric
- theories of writing and learning
- research methods, evaluation methods, and teaching methods
- language and literacy development
- Various MLA, NCTE, and CCCC guidelines and position statements
- local and national developments in writing instruction
- writing, publishing, and presenting at conferences. (Hult et al. 1992)

Given these precise requirements, it is conceivable that a faculty developer whose expertise and training include professional development and preparation to lead teaching and learning centers might not also have the additional training identified by the described requirements above. That said, such training should not impede the ability for faculty developers to collaborate with WPAs who do possess this training. Put simply, one should not expect faculty development centers to possess authority over rhetoric and composition–trained faculty and experts to develop WAC professional development and outreach. However, it is also conceivable that WPAs like me possess both this training and the expertise to lead teaching and learning centers, making such partnerships attainable.

Perhaps another reason why WAC and faculty development partnerships have remained separate is because rhetoric and composition specialists have historically seen teaching and learning centers as a threat to WAC's programmatic existence, therefore seeing faculty development outreach as a threat to WAC efforts and not as an opportunity. Barbara Walvoord's cautions in her 1996 essay "The Future of WAC" that the emergence of teaching and learning centers poses a real threat to WAC budgets. She describes this threat in the following way:

I believe that the most likely scenario over the coming decade is for future education reform programs to coexist in a shifting kaleidoscope, programs disappearing as they can no longer draw funds or faculty, and programs arising. The fluctuations will be encouraged by the funding sources groups—grants and administrators—which still favor innovation . . . [One] space will be the increasingly popular "teaching/learning" centers. These centers may become relatively permanent, endowed or line-item offices . . . and fund initiatives for student learning. Centers may be able to because they are not tied to any particular program but can ride the newest innovations. But alternatively, these centers may tie up existing funding for development, allow the university to claim it values student learning, be ignored by most faculty (Austin), and prevent more effective faculty development from arising. (69)

Despite these fears, there has not been a systematic trend for teaching and learning centers to replace WAC programs, as many WAC programs continue to operate while teaching and learning centers also continue to exist. In a twenty-first-century context, to what degree any budgetary cuts from WAC programming can be attributed to teaching and learning centers remains unclear. Contrarily, shrinking budgets across higher education make it all the more appealing for WAC and faculty development centers to collaborate and build partnerships, as both may potentially pull together resources or work collaboratively to seek external sources of funding.

DIRECT PARTNERSHIPS BETWEEN FACULTY DEVELOPMENT AND WAC CENTERS AND PROGRAMS

In the book *Naming What We Know: Threshold Concepts in Writing Studies*, editors Linda Adler-Kassner and Elizabeth Wardle (2016) identify several concepts essential to understanding the work of writing studies, identifying WAC and faculty development as two key threshold concepts. Their volume further makes explicit and direct connections between WAC and faculty development opportunities. In Adler-Kassner and Majewski's contribution, "Extending the Invitation: Threshold Concepts, Professional Development, and Outreach," the authors note: "In many WAC programs, leaders strategically begin with a focus on writing to learn rather than the production of formal, disciplinary-based writing" (2016, 28). They further indicate: "Whether through faculty development, departmental, or individual consulting, or through shared writing assessment activities, many WAC programs try to reveal the complexities of student writing and the difficulties students experience learning to write across different courses and curricula" (286).

Throughout the chapter, Adler-Kassner and Majewski more directly link WAC outreach and faculty development as key threshold concepts that are intimately tied to one another in ways that affirm the expertise that WAC specialists bring when engaging faculty through the study and teaching of writing. With regard to using faculty development as a systematic threshold concept for campus-wide outreach, they contend:

> While this consideration begins with definitions of a discipline's threshold concepts—what we can think of as a first layer of expertise—it quickly leads to a second layer, expertise associated with knowledge about how to learn and represent threshold concepts (such as how to select, interpret, and use evidence in a discipline). The argument here, then, is that the discussions about threshold concepts are particularly productive starting points for professional development precisely because faculty are invested in their disciplines. (254)

What is also essential to understanding the relationships between WAC outreach and faculty development is the idea of self-efficacy, a concept that is central to the success of faculty development centers (290). One critical way to enhance self-efficacy among faculty is to affirm their authority as experts in their fields of study. What is most useful, though, about Adler-Kassner and Majewski's connections between faculty development and WAC is that faculty may come together to share their expertise: WAC practitioners affirm the expertise of faculty to share knowledge of their fields, while faculty affirm the WAC practitioner's expertise in providing professional development in the teaching of writing. As they simply put it: "For many WAC specialists . . . , helping faculty members embrace this threshold concept is central to faculty development and curricular transformation" (278). Potentially, faculty development centers can become one location or space to facilitate this sharing of knowledge.

In *Creating the Future of Faculty Development: Learning from the Past, Understanding the Present,* Mary Deane Sorcinelli, Ann E. Austin, and Pamela Eddy make direct references to WAC intellectual work and collaborations. In a 2001–2002 survey of topics important to offer, faculty developers identified WAC initiatives as one of the top eight programs needed in faculty development programming, with a moderate number of those surveyed currently offering WAC programming. Sorcinelli, Austin, and Eddy further trace a decline in faculty development programming in relation to WAC. While in the mid-1980s WAC workshops were cited as the most frequently offered faculty development services, recent findings indicate that "the importance of writing across the curriculum . . . was not matched by the extent of activities offered" (2006, 89). One exception to this finding was that smaller liberal arts institutions offer more WAC programming than research and doctoral institutions. They attribute this finding to "the fact that faculty development programs at small liberal arts colleges often collaborate with faculty and students to advance students' abilities in oral and written communication skills" (96). While this research has become dated, it is still important today to emphasize the fact that faculty development centers can be seen as spaces for WAC professional development workshops and thus have a specific role or space within faculty development work and operations.

When considering writing assessment of student learning outcomes, Gudrun Willett and colleagues have more recently identified the role of faculty development centers as central to the work that instructors do when assessing students' writing. From their perspective, "faculty development was understood to mean specific workshops or assessment activities linked to pedagogy that serve as a goal-oriented curriculum for faculty" (21). As they explain, while faculty development is identified through workshops and activities, their understanding of WAC included a formalized programmatic structure, noting: "Because both campuses boast long-standing programs in WAC, regular workshops open to faculty in all disciplines are a mainstay" (21) The formal connections between WAC and faculty development included workshops on developing rubrics to assess portfolios of student writing across disciplines and "specific faculty development events that stressed adaptation of the rubric to learning outcomes in departmental and course-level contexts" (21). Clearly, there is a possibility for a stronger and explicit sense of collaboration between faculty developers and WAC participants, a sort of partnership that should be encouraged across institutions; however, without a central location or hub, it is less clear to what extent these collaborations are sustainable long-term once the assessment workshops, assessment activities, data collection, and results have concluded. Thus, I wonder to what extent faculty development centers and WAC programs can engage in sustained collaborations and partnerships beyond specific activities that have starting and ending dates.

An extended discussion of findings and collaborations between WAC programs and faculty development centers is offered in the book by William Condon and colleagues, *Faculty Development and Student Learning: Assessing the Connections*. Additional benefits from creating stronger partnerships between WAC programming and faculty development include the ability to transform pedagogy and students' achievement of additional learning outcomes besides those related to written communication. Condon and coauthors reveal that not only did WAC faculty participants' classes outperform those classes with faculty who did not participate in WAC workshops, but also, and perhaps more importantly, faculty who worked on improving written communication outcomes also improved critical thinking outcomes as well (2016, 109). The authors further contend:

> While writing and critical thinking are not necessarily related competenc-es . . . WAC workshops often address ways faculty assignments can elicit better thinking, as well as better writing, especially when the same faculty developers who ran the Critical Thinking Project also facilitate the WAC workshops . . . Each lends efficacy to the other, and the real beneficiaries are the students, whose improved learning outcomes established useful-ness of the original faculty development. (109)

A few concepts are noteworthy about Condon and colleagues' findings from WAC and faculty development outreach at both Carleton College and Washington State University. First, students' performances were im-proved by both faculty participation in WAC workshops and additional faculty development workshops that included critical thinking. Second, because these collaborations were in closer proximity, participants and facilitators were able to attend both workshops and adopt pedagogies and assessment practices that targeted multiple areas of student learn-ing outcomes within the same course. The data moreover reveal that students made gains in multiple areas as opposed to only in single areas targeted one at a time. Third, cross-collaborations and initiatives can more adequately enhance faculties' self-efficacies when campus-wide outreach and partnerships are developed, as opposed to those created in different units with separate divisions of labor. In other words, when there is a concerted, campus-wide effort to focus on teaching and learn-ing, as opposed to designating different fields of study for providing professional development on specific teaching and learning practices, faculty begin to identify a unit that values teaching and learning as cen-tral to the institution's mission or vision and prioritizes resources in a way that centralizes teaching and learning and not a single skill or dis-cipline of study.

Zemliansky and Berry (2017) also identify specific collaborations between faculty development activities and WAC in their work with teaching faculty to incorporate more writing in their engineering courses. That said, their understanding of faculty development is limited to a program "designed and taught by members of a WAC program" (308). Put simply, faculty development and WAC are conflated into a single program or set of professional development activities for the purpose of their work with engineering faculty. Such a fact potentially sees faculty development more as one's individual professional development activities, as opposed to faculty development being recognized as a central location or hub for faculty to collaborate across units. Despite a formal structure for a faculty development center to ensure sustainability after completion of the project, Zemliansky and Berry's reported findings do suggest that participants from the program have remained in touch, but the extent of their continued contact was not revealed (313). As most faculty development scholarship shows, though, formal follow-up meetings and debriefing sessions are essential to sustaining the impact of teaching innovations and transformations across the institution (Sullivan et al. 2016).

Unlike the previous references in this section, Carol Rutz and coauthors' (2012) discussion of faculty development and WAC partnerships specifically identifies the direct role of faculty development and teaching and learning centers in helping instructors teach and assess student writing. For them, faculty development programs and teaching and learning centers played an integral role in creating and designing WAC workshops and professional brownbags on teaching practices (43). Their findings further identify the specific value to participants of sustained collaborations: "they reported the following benefits: enjoying the faculty-development experience, forging new or better friendships, increasing opportunities for collaboration, gaining support, establishing better agreement on a shared liberal arts mission, and learning a shared language about and approaches to teaching and learning" (46). With regard to direct collaboration, both institutions, Carleton College and Washington State University, "have long-standing writing-across-the-curriculum programs that require cross-curricular faculty development" (41).

While this section has identified some direct partnerships between faculty development centers and WAC programs, and while I offer faculty development centers as a central location for these partnerships, readers may question why WAC programmatic centers might not be a useful site for stronger collaboration. The short answer to this question lies in the potential for faculty development centers, centers that typically house *all* teaching and learning activities, to reach wider audiences; in contrast, WAC programs, despite their outreach endeavors, are perceived as aligning mainly to English studies. Fairly or not, even when WAC centers and programs are housed outside of English departments with the purpose of serving an entire institution, their roles in providing outreach and professional development are still too often misinterpreted. As Adler-Kassner and Majewski also indicate, today, dozens of writing-intensive and other WAC programs in universities large and small stand as a testament to the gains that have been made in accepting this threshold concept and acting on it. But misunderstanding continues, and a lack of knowledge about the history of writing instruction and its increasing distance from subjects not associated with rhetoric, English, grammar, and literature doesn't help (Russell 1992). . . . Writing may still be associated with certain groups of people and certain academic interests. (2016, 282)

Long before the publication of *Threshold Concepts* (Adler-Kassner and Wardle 2016), advice on developing WAC programs from the ground up cautioned against an overreliance on English studies faculty. As previously referenced in this chapter, Sandler advises WAC program developers not to depend too much on English faculty (38), but also suggests that WAC programs link more to "concepts to improved teaching rather than improved writing" (39). An emphasis more on teaching than on writing provides a fruitful opportunity for collaborations with teaching and learning centers. Sandler's discussion of the "faculty development workshop" earlier in the chapter further identifies the essential role of faculty development as a foundation for WAC outreach and program creation (35).

While writing is often associated with certain disciplines, faculty development centers have traditionally been transdisciplinary. Because faculty development centers are often where the institution houses teaching and learning, therefore offering professional development and resources on pedagogy across disciplines, they often serve as a go-to location for advice and support for teaching. In fact, one reason I became involved in faculty development was because a dean of a college approached our office of faculty development for support and resources on Writing to Learn, perceiving that office as the appropriate location for professional development. At the time, the director and associate director reached out to me to facilitate this workshop because they valued my expertise and training in the teaching of writing. While quite a few faculty in rhetoric and composition (myself included) questioned why the dean would reach out to our office of faculty development in the first place, I now understand why a dean would go to a center that houses teaching and learning activities to facilitate a teaching and learning activity, albeit one closely aligned with writing pedagogy. Nonetheless, an example such as the one offered here emphasizes how faculty development and WAC collaborations can align and work more strongly together for an institution's collective good.

The previous example leads to another reason why faculty development centers might be a useful location for WAC programmatic outreach: centers designed in ways that cross disciplinary boundaries are often those in the best positions to break down silos. As previously referenced, WAC centers are often misleadingly aligned with the work of English studies, and therefore, faculty continue to hold misconceptions about their authority to teach students to write outside of English. As also acknowledged, I recognize that this is a misconception that WAC practitioners and rhetoric and composition scholars must continue to debunk, and thus, I do not suggest that simply collaborating with a faculty development center will automatically debunk these misconceptions. Nor am I suggesting that WAC programs cease to exist as a separate unit and instead be absorbed into teaching and learning centers. Much WAC scholarship provides recommendations for the personnel and resources necessary to develop WAC program budgets and units (Walvoord 1996; Sandler 2000), advice to which I firmly subscribe. I believe WAC programs can and should include designated units, budgets, and staffing; however, being a stand-alone unit does not preclude one from collaborating with a faculty development center that houses teaching and learning activities. That said, WAC as a distinct unit could potentially be structured under the umbrella of a larger center for both faculty development and teaching and learning, thus enhancing both collaboration and communication, but it is essential that one not conflate the units entirely. Regardless of the structure under which WAC and faculty development centers operate, both play essential roles in providing professional development related to the teaching and learning of written literacy.

Up until this point, I have not referenced sources that point to specific locations or sites for these partnerships; I have simply suggested faculty development centers as a potential site that can break down silos of departments by advocating cross-disciplinary collaborations. Perhaps the most explicit discussion of WAC and faculty development collaborations is Artze-Vega and colleagues' 2013 article, "Privileging Pedagogy: Composition, Rhetoric, and Faculty Development," where the authors do point to locations for collaboration. One author, in fact, acknowledges the seeking out of faculty who "'straddle the border between—or, perhaps more appropriately, move between' [faculty development and WAC]" (162). From their perspective, rhetoric and composition expertise "provides uniquely valuable preparation for faculty development careers" (163). They also identify the necessity of breaking silos, a skill they associate with WPAs, as essential to fostering such collaborations (170).

While rhetoric and composition training, especially with regard to WPA work, can provide preparation for faculty development careers, the authors further suggest that rhetoric and composition can benefit from having faculty developers and teaching and learning centers as allies:

> Because faculty developers have a responsibility to read widely about teaching and learning, we encounter resources that can offer insight into the research directly related to the teaching of writing . . . Beyond this general congruence, however, we believe that faculty development research into teaching and learning will offer specific uses for WPAs and other comp/rhet scholars who wish to improve program teaching and learning. (172)

The article moves forward with identifying several insights from faculty development research and scholarship that enhance the work of WPAs. These range from student motivation to the learning that students acquire across disciplines beyond writing. Essentially, the article examines the ways in which WAC programs and faculty development centers can learn from each other by building stronger alliances. Artze-Vega and coauthors indicate that "as many WPAs have found, building a strong program often means building institutional allies, and in fact one of the faculty developer's first duties [is] to 'build a relationship, not a case' (Jensen 2002), because the faculty developers' essential move is to 'work collaboratively'" (173). As far as specific proposals or conclusions, the authors agree that faculty development training should be provided in graduate-level coursework offered within and beyond rhetoric and composition (176). They also recommend that in addition to coursework,

> institutional structures include opportunities in faculty development. Developing internships with CTLs [Centers for Teaching and Learning] or within WAC programs [serves as a] structural way to provide graduate students exposure to faculty work. Perhaps more radically, the terms and expectations teaching assistantship positions might be configured to include activities. Rather than asking graduate students to teach first-year composition for their whole graduate careers, we might build on encouraging experienced teaching assistants to provide structured and instructional feedback for newer graduate teaching assistants, those in other disciplines. . . . What might our departments and graduate programs oriented TAs to theories of teaching adult learners, treated disciplinary apprentices, and gave them a wider range of teaching experiences? (176)

As discussed in chapter 1, where I shared how my experience working as a mentor in the program at my institution that provides professional development for graduate teaching assistants across disciplines was a starting point for my interests in faculty development, a model very similar to what Artze-Vega and coauthors propose above, faculty development centers offer graduate students in rhetoric and composition additional opportunities to explore teaching and learning beyond both first-year writing and rhetoric and composition as a discipline at large. In addition, the authors' discussion is perhaps the closest one gets to understanding the structural connections between WAC programs and centers for faculty development and teaching and learning. Both can be seen as separate institutional units that work very closely and collaboratively with each other, whether through formal initiatives or additional partnerships. With these collaborative roles, WAC specialists and WPAs are provided with opportunities to travel between both faculty development and WAC spaces, and "define their own roles in relation to these two fields" (177).

As I understand it, these roles may potentially suggest inhabiting both spaces, shifting back and forth between the two spaces, or merging both spaces into a singular location. The ways in which these roles are defined greatly depend on the institution's existing structures. As previously acknowledged in chapter 1, because my institution does not have a formal WAC program, I'm interested in identifying opportunities for WAC outreach under our office of faculty development, who has already done significant work with Writing to Learn outreach. I am also interested in such an approach to facilitate stronger collaboration and partnership between the two fields in ways that reinforce common interests in teaching and learning. As Artze-Vega and colleagues suggest, both units have a lot to offer each other, and these partnerships can greatly enrich and enhance the professional development WPAs offer in the teaching and learning of writing. Of course, such a structure is not appropriate everywhere; however, given shrinking budgets, it was more feasible for me to propose WAC activities to an administration than it was to propose a brand-new program or institute with a full budget, especially since "we need higher education leadership to sustain this focus" (177).

THE DIVERSITY AND INCLUSION WORK OF FACULTY DEVELOPMENT: LEVERAGING WRITING EXPERTISE FOR THE INSTITUTION

As previously acknowledged in chapter 1, increasing numbers of women of color came to me for support when I became associate director of OFD. Many of them desired advice for navigating the day-to-day departmental politics and microaggressions they experienced by colleagues in their departments. Others needed advice on how to delicately navigate departments and institutions as women of color seeking tenure and promotion. While I initially set out to do primarily WAC-related work, I recognized the need to develop diversity and inclusion programming, a passion that I had previously pursued through institutional committee

work and disciplinary scholarship. As I talked with women of color, I
shared my own stories of navigating departmental politics and microaggressions. On a few occasions, I directed them to the scholarship I'd
published on my own experiences with intersectional identity politics.
On other occasions, I simply shared my initial experiences with finding
women of color with whom to connect on campus. As a new assistant
professor, when I first went to well-meaning colleagues in my department seeking names of other African American women around the
university with whom I could solicit advice for seeking tenure, I was
told on multiple occasions that there were too few to find. It wasn't
until I shared my experiences with my hairdresser that I was put in
touch with the many African American women on campus. There were
far more than a few; it was just that these women did not navigate the
same networks of my colleagues in English. And when I connected with
them finally, several indicated that they had no idea there were African
American women in the English department at all! Such an experience
greatly underscores the need to expand institutional networks by breaking department silos. Moreover, such an experience is also reflective of
the need to expand diversity and inclusion work beyond English departments and writing programs.

OFD's Seminar on Teaching Inclusivity: A Site for Diversity, Equity and Inclusion Work

OFD, our primary teaching and learning center, is now housed under
WMUx, a unit that centralizes faculty development and instructional
design under the same unit for faculty to access all teaching and learning and pedagogical campus resources. Prior to this move in 2020, however, OFD was a stand-alone unit that reported to an associate provost
for assessment and undergraduate studies. Later in this volume, I will
build upon the discussion of centralization in this chapter and the next;
here, however, I will discuss programming that was housed separately
because WMUx did not yet exist. My experience with navigating institutional networks shaped one of the first diversity and inclusion programs
I developed for OFD: the Summer Seminar on Teaching Inclusivity.
During fall 2016, I began planning a two-day workshop on diversity and
inclusion programming. Day one would focus on diversity and inclusion
pedagogy across the disciplines, while day two would focus on ways to
practice inclusivity in the workplace. The first seminar ran on June 13 and
14, 2017, and included breakout sessions for teaching culturally relevant
pedagogies in the humanities, social sciences, and STEM disciplines;

adopting LGBTQ+-friendly classroom practices; diversity and inclusion in the teaching of writing; working with students with disabilities; and faculty and student panels that provided attendees with advice for avoiding microaggressions and on other culturally sensitive practices, topics very similar to those discussed in Bergmann's article about white privilege (2008, 539). More recent works also consider the roles of writing centers with anti-racist pedagogies and faculty development (Martini and Webster 2021).

Day two's programming included a panel of allies and historically oppressed and underrepresented faculty on their experiences with microaggressions in their home departments, followed by breakout sessions for navigating being the only underrepresented minority in your department, a presentation inspired by Kerry Ann Rockquemore's presentation "What to Do When You're the Only ____ in the Department," facilitated at the 2016 annual Faculty Women of Color in the Academy Conference (see http://www.cpe.vt.edu/fwca/), a conference I attended prior to doing faculty development work. Other breakout sessions provided resources for early-career scholars pursuing research, scholarship, and creative activity opportunities, as well as resources for graduate students and contingent faculty navigating the job market in relation to their own subject positions. During the lunch hour on both days, various organizations across campus provided resource tables for faculty and instructors regarding the support services offered by their offices to support inclusive work.

The first seminar drew over fifty participants, including senior administrators, faculty, staff, part-time instructors, and graduate students (WMU OFD 2018), which is extraordinary for a summer event on a unionized campus where faculty are not expected or required to participate in, work at, or attend campus-sponsored events during the summer. As standard, OFD conducts evaluations for all of its programming and includes results in its annual report. The surveys conducted for the Seminar on Teaching Inclusivity in 2017 reflect a 38 percent response rate for day one, and a 28 percent response rate for day two (these response rates increased to 48 percent on day one and 30 percent on day two in 2018; feedback from the 2018 Seminar will be discussed later in this chapter). Survey results from participants revealed that on a scale of 1 to 5, with 1 being "not at all welcoming" and 5 being "very welcoming," respondents averaged 4.3 for the seminar being a welcoming and inclusive environment on day one; respondents averaged 4.86 for day two. To be clear, surveys are simply used as an opportunity for participants to provide feedback to improve OFD programs; while the results gathered from this feedback are included in our annual reports identifying a summary of activities, these results are not intended to be representative of any specific population. That said, when asked what specific pedagogical strategies participants took from day one, respondents identified the following takeaways:

- Thinking about writing, rhetoric, and language differently in relation to what good and bad writing look like
- Thinking about equality issues differently when giving feedback to students
- Providing more support to international students
- Being more intentional about course design, creating the classroom culture from the start
- Adopting preferred pronoun policies
- Revising syllabi with more inclusive language
- Being more mindful and sensitive to students' experiences. (see Appendix H)

When asked for suggestions for improving day one, respondents identified the following strategies, among others:

- The need for speakers to use microphones, and to model ADA practices
- The desire for more concrete activities that instructors can use in their own classrooms
- To establish more training around microaggressions and implicit biases
- To offer additional programming during the academic year on these topics and not just in the summer. (see Appendix H)

With regard to day two's programming, respondents identified the following takeaways:

- The importance of peer support to survive at PWIs
- The necessity of time management/work/life strategies to enhance research and scholarly productivity
- The need to network beyond the department
- The need to encourage colleagues to participate and attend workshops like the seminar
- To help increase empathy and understanding.
- Seeking out mentors for support. (see Appendix H)

With regard to suggestions for improvement, the following:

- Increasing attendance with senior leadership: Many expressed concerns that more administrators on fiscal-year contracts should have been in attendance in comparison to faculty who are not required to be on campus during the summer.

- Requiring administrators, deans, chairs, and directors attend something similar and provide them with a summary of comments shared over the two days.

- Defining diversity and inclusive terminology more perhaps with a handout or glossary of commonly used terms.

- Connecting scholarly productivity and job market workshops more to diversity and inclusion work. Some respondents did not quite understand the connections between promoting inclusive institutional practices and generally preparing participants for career success. (Appendix H)

Survey findings reflect the ways in which WAC outreach and diversity and inclusion pedagogy are critical to institutional progress and professional development. Much of day one's feedback emphasized the connections between implicit bias on language and the ways in which faculty respond to student writing. It is important to emphasize here that the session on inclusive practices in the teaching of writing was facilitated by me, particularly since I desired to make more overt institutional connections between the work that WPAs do with respect to linguistic diversity outside of the discipline and, by proxy, outside of the writing program. In chapter 6 of *Afrocentric Teacher-Research*, I critiqued composition's failure to effectively make the case for linguistic diversity beyond the discipline, asserting and recommending the following:

> To develop a more persuasive discourse, composition can take practical steps that seek to correct inequalities associated with language policies in our higher education institutions by aligning the struggle for language rights with our institution's mission and policy statements, particularly those that emphasize the need for diversity. As I have argued . . . the field must emphasize the sophisticated processes and competencies associated with multilingual learners and communicators . . . We can achieve this by first aligning our programmatic learning objectives and mission statements with the broader university mission statement. (122)

Specifically during my workshop, Inclusivity and the Teaching of Writing, I began by providing participants with practical examples of how speakers practice linguistic prejudice daily, showing them a collage of web-based Creative Commons images to illustrate the biases and judgments made against speakers of other Englishes and languages varieties. Figure 3.1 reflects this collage:[1]

After displaying practical examples, I shared a few myths about how English works and the linguistic prejudices, judgments, and hypocrisies

---

1. All images meet Creative Commons licensing standards.

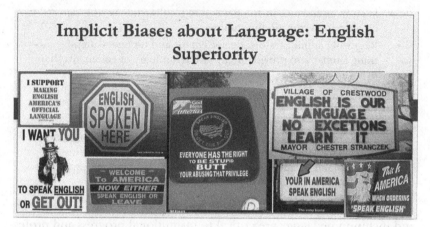

Figure 3.1. Linguistic Prejudice Collage.

often based on these myths, grounded in material from the blog post I published in 2015, "Languages, Dialects, and the Myth of Edited American English." Analyzing these myths educated participants against the assumption that languages and language varieties carry prestige and against the existence of "broken English." After reviewing these myths, I introduced participants to the CCCC resolution on Students' Right to Their Own Language, a position statement with which no participant had any familiarity. The workshop concluded with specific strategies for responding and evaluating the writing of speakers of other Englishes and language varieties. The practices in this workshop are also consistent with recommendations that composition scholars present

> scholarly research establishing the legitimacy of Ebonics [and all language varieties] . . . If organizations such as the National Council of Teachers of English [NCTE], the CCCC, or International Reading Association [IRA] can (1) communicate to an audience that includes parents, community leaders, and . . . administrators and (2) provide empirical data that supports success with learning about Ebonics and other languages and dialects beside [Standard English], composition can move one step further toward persuasion. (Perryman-Clark 2013, 113)

While facilitating this workshop, multiple participants responded by questioning why they had never heard of CCCC and why they had never learned about these myths; others were disillusioned about how problematic their evaluative practices had been in the past, regretting thereby doing a disservice to students. Such an instance, while anecdotal, greatly underscores the necessity of both WAC and diversity and inclusion workshops. Furthermore, additional feedback from the entire Summer

Seminar on Teaching Inclusivity points to the need for expanding this programming more continuously, something OFD began to do with the creation of the Teaching Inclusivity Series that would take place during the following academic year.

The Teaching Inclusivity Series expanded on topics of equity, inclusion, and access and entailed two-hour workshops on topics including creating ADA accessible documents, handouts, and materials; creating trans-friendly pedagogical materials; overcoming microaggressions in one's department; and locating networks of support beyond the department. One workshop, A Response to Charlottesville, was developed in response to the neo-Nazi rally that left one counterprotestor killed and many others injured. At the time, faculty contacted OFD because they desired resources about how to address hate speech in the classroom, how to work with students who adopt neo-Nazi attitudes, and what their rights and responsibilities were as faculty when teaching these students. As such, OFD worked collaboratively with WMU's shared governance organizations, the WMU chapter of the Association of American University Professors (AAUP) and the Faculty Senate, who provided resources as they pertained to faculty rights and responsibilities concerning academic freedom, while OFD shared pedagogical resources. While unintended, the workshop conversation turned to strategies for responding to students' writing when they produce opinions and ideologies consistent with anti-inclusive practices. As such, as one of the facilitators of this workshop, I provided attendees with ways to develop rhetorical approaches to respond to students' ideologies. We discussed providing resources on logical fallacies and other ways to respond to errors in reasoning and the cultural logic associated with certain ideologies without strictly attacking students' core beliefs. We also discussed strategies for using the categories of including evidence and avoiding errors in logic and reasoning as part of rubric evaluation, so students could align their grade with the criteria and not with the instructor's philosophical beliefs. The Response to Charlottesville workshop provides just another case for why WAC work is diversity work and how teaching and learning centers make these sorts of collaborations possible. Such a workshop also suggests another opportunity for WAC specialists to provide rhetorical training and education for how faculty can navigate students' beliefs and the ways they write about them in content-based courses.

Based on feedback from the 2017 Seminar on Teaching Inclusivity, several respondents requested a web-based list of additional resources to consult during the academic year. Because the discussion of student writing was addressed across some of the sessions besides the one I facilitated, I added a list of rhetoric and composition resources as they connected to diversity and inclusion (see https://wmich.edu/facultydevelopment/inclusivityresources). Some of these resources included bibliographic entries of articles published by Collin Craig and me on the relationship between intersectional identity politics and microaggressions. Others included resources on linguistic diversity for second-language writers and speakers of other Englishes. In addition, we raffled off several books that addressed themes from the two-day workshops and included many rhetoric and composition books as connected to these themes. We were able to raffle off *Antiracist Writing Ecologies* by Asao B. Inoue, *Mad at School: Rhetorics of Mental Disability and Academic Life* by Margaret Price, and *Students' Right to Their Own Language: A Critical Sourcebook* by David E. Kirkland, Austin Jackson, and me. What is interesting about these raffles is the fact that participants were able to choose which books they had a chance to win, thus emphasizing the strong interest on writing topics despite the seminar's primary focus on diversity and inclusion.

As previously discussed in this chapter, response rates for feedback increased in 2018, though the total number of participants remained at fifty. Similarly, there were no increases in the number of associate deans and department chairs who attended the seminar from 2017. Also similarly to 2017, no deans, associate provosts, provosts, or vice presidents were in attendance, though two associate deans did attend. In response to feedback from the previous year, 2018's programming included a panel of dean's-level and other senior office administrators (department chair and beyond) on overcoming implicit biases in tenure and promotion. The panel was composed of current and past associate deans, department chairs, labor relations officers, and full professors who had served on tenure and promotions committees; however, only one associate dean and one department chair were in the audience as attendees. Survey feedback specific to this panel indicated the following comments from the day's presentations:

- "The extent of bias in the tenure and promotion process."
- "Tenure is a bitch."
- "Strategies for T&P Reviewers—stimulated ideas on how my department could approach the T&P committee members/expectations."
- "All the presenters were good. I applaud them for sharing their stories. Diversity and inclusion training should be made mandatory for every division and department with some form of accountability required for the leadership." (WMU OFD 2018a)

Additional criticisms in response to the 2018 Seminar further emphasized the necessity for faculty development diversity and inclusion programming to fully address microaggressions and the challenges associated with institutional buy-in. One respondent shared the following concerns about the emphasis on participants sharing their stories about microaggressions and the politics associated with sufficiently covering every population that has experienced oppression:

> There was a little bit too much focus on sharing examples of microaggressions. I think this focuses too much on the problems. I would like to see more focus on specific solutions—constructive next steps. (I started to think our students were presented as "victims" a little too much. There's a lot of great stuff going on here on campus.) What about a panel of "heroes?" That is, having folks who've really stepped up when an issue faced them in class or in a department and how they handled it . . . what went well, what didn't go well, what they'd do next time could be interesting and problem-solving focused. There was some focus on this, but perhaps even more focus on it would be useful. Also, it would be helpful to share more data on the problems and effective solutions as opposed to perceptions of personal experiences. Finally, helping us better understand terminology we should use, issues of gender pronouns, etc. would be helpful. I understand that the microaggressions are important to share to increase awareness, but I think we have to be careful about massaging the problem too much. (For example, when one panelist said he hadn't really encountered any problems, he was pushed to think further about it to come up with one. How come we weren't celebrating that he had had a positive experience? It was almost like we were looking for a problem.) Also, there was one panelist with a disability, but I would like to see more focus on disability. Diversity is a very broad topic and encompasses more than racial issues and gender issues . . . (veteran status, children from foster care, first generation . . .).

Based on this criticism, it is difficult not to be too defensive when rebutting the assumption that the program focused mostly on racial and gender oppressions. That said, I've included a copy of the 2017 program for days one and two to provide readers with the ways that OFD attempted to represent as many oppressed populations as possible. The following reflects day one's programming:

Summer Seminar for Teaching Inclusivity Program

June 13 and 14, 2017

Fetzer Center

   Day One: Creating Safe Spaces for Diverse Learners in the Classroom

      9:00 Welcome and Remarks—Room 2020

      9:15–10:30 *Q/A Session on Teaching Diversity and Safe Spaces for Students*—Room 2020

Susan Freeman, associate professor and chair, Department of Gender and Women's Studies

Beverly Vandiver, professor, Department of Counseling Education and Counseling psychology

Jill Hermann-Wilmarth, professor, Department of Teaching, Learning, and Educational Studies

10:30–10:45 Break

10:45–12:00 *Concurrent Breakout Session*—Pedagogical Strategies and Activities to Teach Inclusivity (Choose ONE)

Humanities: Room 2020
Sue Ellen Christian, professor, School of Communication

STEM: Room 2030
Pamela Hoppe, associate professor, Department of Biological Sciences
NaTasha Schiller, graduate teaching assistant, Department of Biological Sciences

Social Sciences: Room 2040
Douglas Davidson, associate professor, Department of Sociology

12:00–1:00 Lunch: Room 1040/1050
Resource tables for faculty and instructors working with students of diverse backgrounds are featured in the lobby.

Center of Academic Success Programs (CASP)
Randy Ott, director, Center of Academic Success Programs
Shawn L. Tenney and John Scott, Office of Service Learning

Broncos FIRST
Charles Henderson, co-director, Broncos FIRST; professor, Department of Physics
Monica Liggins-Abrams, associate director, Broncos FIRST and CRICPE

LBGT Student Services
Nathan Nguyen, director, Office of Lesbian, Bisexual, Gay and Transgender Student Services

College Migrant Assistance Program
Liliana Salas, coordinator of Services, College Assistance Migrant Program (CAMP), Division of Multicultural Affair

Office of Disability Services
Jayne Fraley-Burgett, director, Office of Disability Services

Bronco Study Zone
Ben Carr, manager, Bronco Study Zone

Student Success Services
Katie Easley, director, Student Success Services

1:00–2:15 *Concurrent Breakout Session*—Implicit Bias and Inclusive Pedagogy (Choose ONE)

Room 2030 Inclusivity and the Teaching of Writing: Pedagogies for Second Language Writers and Speakers of English Language Varieties
Staci Perryman-Clark, associate professor of English; director of First-Year Writing; associate director, Office of Faculty Development
Ila M. Baker, master faculty specialist, Center for English Language and Culture for International Students (CELCIS)
Eva Copija, faculty specialist II, CELCIS

Room 2040. Inclusivity and Access: Teaching Students With Disabilities
Jayne Fraley-Burgett, director, Office of Disability Services

2:15–2:30 Break

2:30–3:30 Q/A Panel on Students' Experiences with Diversity and Inclusion: Room 2020

Moderators:
Sue Stapleton, dean, Graduate College
Dawnielle Simmons, doctoral student, Department of Counseling

Psychology

Student Assembly for Racial Equity and Cultural Inclusion (SAREC)
NaTasha Schiller, graduate teaching assistant, Department of Biological Sciences
Jayne Fraley-Burgett, director, Office of Disability Services

3:30–4:00 Thoughts, Reflections and Book Prize Raffle—Room 2020

Day two's programming was as follows:

Summer Seminar Teaching Inclusivity

June 13 and 14, 2017

Fetzer Center

Day Two: Safe Spaces and Support for Faculty and Instructors

9:00 Welcome and Remarks—Room 2020

9:15–10:30 Q/A with Faculty and Instructors from Underrepresented Groups on Campus—Room 2020
David Paul, faculty specialist I–lecturer, Department of Philosophy
Chien-Juh Gu, associate professor, Department of Sociology
Mariam Konate, associate professor, Department of Gender and Women's Studies

10:30–10:45 Break

10:45–12:00 *Concurrent Breakout Session*—Faculty Support and Ally Development (Choose ONE)
Room 2030 What to Do When You're the Only ____ in Your Department: A Survivor's Guide
Staci Perryman-Clark, associate professor, Department of English; director of First-Year Writing; associate director, Office of Faculty Development

Room 2040 Faculty Diversity Qualitative Study: Fostering Ally
Development and Alliances
Annette N. Hamel, faculty specialist II, school of Communication

12:00–1:00 Lunch—Room 1040/1050 .
Resource tables for faculty and instructors relating to workplace
practices will be featured in the lobby.

WMU AAUP
*Lisa Minnick, president, associate professor of English, Office of
Institutional Equity*
*Felicia Taylor Crawford, director, Title IX Compliance and Title IX
Coordinator*

Professional Instructors Organization (PIO)

1:00–2:15 Q/A Session with Faculty and Instructors on Work/Life
Balance—Room 2020
Brian Gogan, associate professor, Department of English
Cathryn Bailey, professor, Department of Gender and Women's
Studies
Luchara Wallace, associate professor, Department of Special
Education and Literacy Studies
Thomas Kostrzewa, part-time instructor, College of Arts and
Sciences

2:15–2:30 Break

2:30–3:30 *Concurrent Breakout Session*—Research, Scholarship and Creative Activity (Choose ONE)

Room 2030: Faculty and Instructors: Research, Scholarship and
Creative Activity Workshop
*Sherine Obare, professor of Chemistry and Associate Vice President for
Research*

Room 2040: Graduate Students and Prospective Job Seekers

Tony Dennis, director of Recruitment and Retention, Graduate College
3:30–4:00 Thoughts, Reflections and Prize Raffle—Room 2020

While 2018's Seminar on Teaching Inclusivity did not designate
a specific session devoted to the teaching of writing, the humanities
breakout session did include an expanded presentation on ways to
integrate both reading and writing into the classroom. I would argue,
though, that expanded diversity and inclusion conversations, while not
writing-focused, benefit WAC specialists and writing educators. While
WAC outreach is still an OFD priority, as an OFD team we decided
to emphasize a more comprehensive inclusion of as many historically
oppressed populations as possible, especially given the shifts in national
policy on immigration and education under the Trump presidential

administration. At the time of our workshops, OFD determined that a commitment to equity and justice was essential: the future of the Deferred Action for Childhood Arrivals (DACA, a US immigration policy that allows children brought to the US illegally to remain in the US) was uncertain, and there were efforts toward changing Title IX policies for reporting sexual assaults in postsecondary institutions as well as weakening requirements for businesses to comply with the American Disabilities Act (ADA). However, implicit in these discussions was the role of rhetoric in navigating difficult times. While I previously discussed the ways that we can draw on concepts of rhetorical theory to respond to students whose writing is informed by racist and controversial views, similarly, as educators, we can draw on rhetorical principles not only to help students navigate the times but also to help design and implement inclusive policies intended to persuade leadership toward institutional adoption. We can use our own strengths and experiences associated with research, information literacy, critical thinking, and oral and written communication skills (all skills WMU has designated as foundational to a general education curriculum) as transferable to effecting institutional change, supporting our colleagues, and supporting our students to transform and react to public policy. And we can also learn more about how to implement campus-wide practices concerning diversity and inclusion in our own college writing classrooms.

As previously stated, the Teaching Inclusivity Series expanded on topics of equity, inclusion. One workshop, A Response to Charlottesville, was developed in response to faculty who contacted OFD because they desired resources about how to address hate speech in the classroom while encouraging free speech, how to work with students who adopt neo-Nazi attitudes, and what their rights and responsibilities were as faculty when teaching these students. As such, OFD worked collaboratively with WMU's shared governance organizations, the WMU chapter of the Association of American University Professors (AAUP), and the Faculty Senate, who provided resources as they pertained to faculty rights and responsibilities concerning academic freedom, while OFD shared pedagogical resources. While unintended, the workshop conversation turned to strategies for responding to students' writing when they produce opinions and ideologies consistent with anti-inclusive practices. As such, as one of the facilitators of this workshop, I provided attendees with ways to develop rhetorical approaches to respond to students' ideologies. We discussed resources on logical fallacies and other ways to respond to errors in reasoning and the cultural logic associated with certain ideologies without strictly attacking students' core beliefs. We also discussed strategies for including evidence and the avoidance of errors in logic and reasoning as part of rubric evaluation, so students could align their grade with the criteria and not with the instructor's philosophical beliefs. The Response to Charlottesville workshop provides just another case for why WAC work is diversity work and how teaching and learning centers make these sorts of collaborations possible, but it also serves as a reminder of how we consider SRTOL in relation to free speech and views we do not support. Rhetorical education provides us with the opportunity to teach within the limits of free speech. Such a workshop also suggests another opportunity for WAC specialists to provide rhetorical training and education for how faculty can navigate students' beliefs and the ways they write about them in content-based courses.

Upon the conclusion of the third year of the year-long Teaching Inclusivity Series, OFD created a WAC Faculty Fellow position to help develop programming for both WAC initiatives and teaching inclusivity. Even more recently, post-#GeorgeFloyd, OFD was authorized to post a Diversity and Inclusion Faculty Fellow as well. In particular, OFD developed a series of workshops for multiple audiences on international pedagogies and techniques to support speakers of other Englishes. While some of the emphasis pertains to an inclusive classroom climate and environment, there has also been careful attention devoted to the ways in which instructors respond to the writing of international students. After leaving OFD, I plan to continue to facilitate workshops around language rights, student writing, and anti-racist teaching practices.

In addition to working with international students, the teaching inclusivity series has also expanded professional development concerning accessibility, as well as resources for working with students with mental health challenges. While it is clear how such topics pertain to diversity, the case can also be made as to why these topics belong as part of WAC programming. While significant attention has been paid to accessibility and disability studies in rhetoric and composition (Heilker and Yergeau 2011; Price 2011; Yergeau 2013), the connections between this work and WAC program development remain less explored. Document design, in particular how instructors make documents accessible, is a writing issue. Moreover, given the smaller class sizes of writing courses, writing teachers are often the first line of defense on behalf of students when they disclose mental health concerns, and writing teachers are often the first observers of changes in student behavior. Institutionally, WMU has developed first-point-of-contact training for faculty, staff, and advisors to respond to mental health matters. While some of this training has been included as part of the inclusivity series, additional training was provided by a campus mental health coordinator. Topics such as mental health require professional development within both diversity and faculty development programming, and writing specialists both gain and contribute tremendous knowledge to these conversations. With any of these conversations or practices, though, the language that we and our students use is critical, and it behooves faculty and instructors to understand and practice inclusive language. Put simply, SRTOL is not limited solely to writing, but it is intricately woven and transferable to broader discussions of identity and why language matters when affirming identities through inclusive practices. In short, this is what inclusive work could look like at an institution when bridging and leveraging partnerships between what we do as writing educators and what institutional offices and initiatives have to offer.

THE FUTURE OF DIVERSITY AND INCLUSION IN WAC INITIATIVES: UNIVERSITY COLLEGE MODELS FOR CENTRALIZATION

With regard to the work of WAC, our outreach as writing specialists is needed to help those teaching writing in their disciplines accept the fact that first-year writing and other lower-division writing courses do not cure all writing problems; nor do they purport to teach students who write exclusively for just one discipline. My outreach with OFD has taught me that we need to talk more to gain a better understanding of what happens not only within but across writing courses. And we each need to do our part to ensure that our assessment practices are not culturally biased. One strategy teaching and learning centers might use to build partnerships is through the centralization I describe in more depth in the next chapter.

In brief, the process of centralization is one that moves new or existing units under a single structure. Centralized units may have previously been decentralized, or may have been centralized differently (Bray 1999, 202). The process of centralization is not without criticism, however. As Massy argues, "Centralization can disempower those who represent the institution's core competencies, undermining the incentives for productivity and improvement and making accountability for such improvements impossible" (1996, 5). For this reason, institutions are often required to achieve the balance of centralization with decentralized units that require specific measures of accountability. In the next chapter, I will discuss more directly how budget models strike this precise balance.

Through the process of centralization, as previously stated, OFD was moved under the unit WMUx, a unit that merges online education, OFD, and instructional design resources to build upon pedagogical innovation. Simply put, "The methods and approach of WMUx are significantly different from the typical methods and approaches used in academia. Human-centered design, collaboration & inclusion, and translation of meaning and understanding will serve as the core pillars of a different way to solve problems" ("What is WMUx?" 2021). This unit is managed by a vice provost for teaching and learning. While it does not bear the same responsibilities as decentralized units, particularly when it comes to student enrollment, units such as these are required to justify their existence and to demonstrate how they align with the institution's core mission and values.

Also under the purview of the vice provost of teaching and learning is WMU's University College, known as the Merze Tate College. Specifically, the college "is an alliance of services, units, and departments that exist to help empower every student to reach their highest potential and provide them with ways to seize success, thrive in all dimensions of their well-being, and lay the foundation for a prosperous future" ("About Merze Tate College" 2022). What is noteworthy about the college is the specific set of subunits that help build this alliance. The unit houses centralized academic advising, where academic advisors across colleges are trained to employ consistent advising methods and best practices, career and support services for students, academic programs including WMU Essential Studies (general education), and student success services like peer tutoring and study zones, including the campus Writing Center. Named after Merze Tate, the first African American woman to graduate from WMU, its mission seeks to provide comprehensive support to a diverse student body, using exploratory advising and student support programs like the federal TRIO Student Success Programs that target students from historically oppressed populations. While a centralization model like university colleges is outlined more specifically in the last chapter, merging oversight for both instruction and student success under a specific area enables universities to share resources and also form stronger collaborations and alliances with each other.

Working in environments outside of first-year writing has taught me that it is the unique set of transferable skills pertaining to expertise in both rhetoric and composition and diversity and inclusion that has helped me make meaningful contributions to these areas. Here are a few takeaways for the impact of our work and the future of higher education, in particular for enrollment management:

1. **Enrollment recruitment.** One strength of the centralized advising model, as offered through the Merze Tate College, is its ability to recruit students from wider demographics, therefore illustrating that institutional resources are in fact accessible to them. It also enables students to consider exploratory advising resources as support for those who want to access institutions of higher education but are unsure of a major or want to change a major. Despite the fact that many elite private and flagship institutions have increased enrollment over the past decade, enrollment has gone down nearly 5 percent across Michigan's fifteen other public colleges and universities over the last five years (Johnson 2021). Part of this decline in enrollments in the state of Michigan has been explained by the shifting demographics in the state. In particular, the number of high school graduates across the state of Michigan continues to steadily decline (French 2021). As such, there is a smaller pool of Michigan in-state students for public universities to recruit from. Given these shifting demographics, institutions are increasingly recruiting international students and students from out of state. But this is a challenge for regional institutions like WMU. While international enrollment and out-of-state enrollment continued to increase (Western Michigan University 2019), increasing these overall demographic groups has not been sufficient to offset overall enrollment. As such, enrollment managers across institutions and the state are considering ways to develop pipelines between urban public school districts like Detroit Public Schools and their institutions. But looking to both Detroit and international students to boost enrollment means we will be teaching students with multiple racial and linguistic identities, therefore making the work we do with regard to WAC more critical.

2. **Retention.** Pegeen Reichert Powell's scholarship has explored the connections between first-year writing and retention initiatives (Powell 2009). Particularly at WMU, successful completion of first-year writing has been one of the greatest indicators of first-to-second-year retention. Providing an example from another institution, in chapter 6 of *Black Perspectives in Writing Program Administration: From the Margins to the Center*, Adrienne Redding, Jeanne LaHaie, and Jonathan Bush describe ENGL 1050-I, a first-year writing-intensive program that takes students at risk of failure and provides them with intensive one-on-one instruction to successfully complete the course. The developers of this program also discuss the specific demographics of those placed in this program, where 66 percent of participants are nonwhite. From their efforts, their retention rate "increased from 36 percent to 64 percent with the population of students with the highest likelihood of leaving the university, students who would have failed first-year writing" (Redding, LaHaie, Bush, Lockett, Stewart, and Stone 2019, 132). Not only do the authors address retention, but they also address the implications of inclusive language policies for participants and provide examples of students speaking African American language. Obviously the work of WAC extends beyond first-year writing; however, if we are considering first-to-second-year retention, and even retention beyond that, many of these students won't

disappear and will have to encounter writing in other courses. Thus, WAC needs to be ready to address the shifting demographics and their connections to retention. Centralized advising provides institutions with opportunities to build partnerships across colleges and catch students who may fall through the cracks when switching from one major to another. Consistent contact with academic advisors is key for retention.

3. **Student success.** For the purposes of this talk, I will define student success by graduation rates, with WMU's current graduation rate standing at a mere 52 percent. Centralized models that put student support resources like writing centers and peer tutoring under a singular unit enable collaboration between units while also supporting students' progress toward the degree. Obviously retention is connected to graduation, since students must successfully complete first-year writing and perhaps an advanced writing course to graduate. Nationally, the most recent statistics gathered from the National Center for Education Statistics (NCES) indicate that the six-year graduation rate for all "first time in a college" (FTIAC) groups was 41.6 percent; in contrast, African American students only graduated at a 21.5 percent rate in six years (see https://nces.ed.gov/programs/digest/d18/tables/dt18_326.10.asp). Specifically, when considering persistent rates after the third year of postsecondary education, "both Asian and White students had a higher persistence rate than Hispanic (79 percent), Black (69 percent), and American Indian / Alaska Native students (64 percent)" (see https://nces.ed.gov/programs/coe/indicator_tsc.asp).

Here is where WAC specialists are needed when considering the impact of advanced writing courses in relation to persistence, and where campus writing centers can also play a critical role. Some persistence has a great deal to do with available financial aid, as is the case on our campus; regardless, we cannot neatly separate the languages that students bring with them into the classroom from their cultural identities. This means that our advanced- and baccalaureate-level writing classes need to be critically assessed in relation to SRTOL and inclusive practices in the classroom. This is particularly critical because it is at these levels where faculty are often content experts and not writing specialists. It is this precise critical audience we must address through faculty development and WAC programming.

Let's dig a bit deeper for a moment and look at graduating senior data in relation to both writing and inclusivity instruction. Of participating institutions respond to the National Survey of Student Engagement (NSSE) in 2018, 85 percent of students reported experiences with that they had made at least some improvements in their ability to write clearly and effectively, while 91 percent reported that they improved in their abilities to understand people of other backgrounds (NSSE 2018). These results are significant because both written communication skills and diversity-related knowledge are both identified as key skills for graduating seniors to acquire prior to entering the workforce.

While NSSE data reference students' perceptions of what they have learned, they are also critical data that help us see how students understand and value what they have learned and what we have taught them. SRTOL potentially becomes one of the most effective tools for college instructors of all fields to help students understand the relationships between disciplinary conventions, language conventions, and equity and privilege. Bringing SRTOL to a broader audience, then, enables WAC specialists to equip instructors with tools for writing instruction while also emphasizing student engagement in relation to inclusive education.

Beyond the work of student success, such work has implications for how we provide professional development for faculty in workplace interactions with other faculty. As previously stated, faculty development can benefit from the rhetorical education we provide, and as a discipline, we can benefit from the diversity and inclusion training provided through faculty development initiatives. For instance, since my departure from OFD, the campus has invested in professional development built around diversity and inclusion; however, it has yet to make the same investment to increase resources for WAC, although it has provided the infrastructure for faculty development and student support services. Following the murder of George Floyd in 2020, WMU created a Racial Justice Advisory Committee (RJAC), which is charged with serving as "catalyst for creating a more inclusive environment and equitable structures at Western Michigan University" ("Racial Justice Advisory Committee" 2021). The committee is broken down into the following subcommittees:

- Equitable Physical Campus Environment
- Equitable Programs
- Reporting Incidents and Equitable Policies and Practices
- Recruiting and Retaining Faculty/Staff of Color
- Recruiting and Retaining Students of Color
- Training Faculty and Staff
- Training Students ("Racial Justice Advisory Committee" 2021)

As previously noted in this chapter, the work of WAC and diversity and inclusion has a range of implications for recruiting and retaining students. The work that began from OFD's Teaching Inclusivity Series also shows that recruiting and retaining faculty and staff of color is critical to the operations of healthy institutions. WAC specialists can all benefit from having professional development around how we recruit and retain BIPOC faculty. Moreover, we can offer our own professional development with WAC to assist in diversity and inclusion efforts to train faculty and staff, as also discussed previously in this chapter. The key to doing racial justice work to support diversity and inclusion lies in building relationships and cross-institutional collaborations. The campus-wide Racial Justice Advisory Committee provides us with another institutional point for strengthening campus-wide collaboration.

The data on campus diversity climates further provide both opportunities and areas for growth and improvement in the areas of diversity and racial justice, as explained in the RJAC climate study:

- For example, at most, 50 percent of the faculty, staff and students who completed the survey felt multiculturalism or inclusion are core values of WMU's mission.
- Respondents felt campus is most welcoming to Caucasian/white individuals and men. For other groups, including people from communities of color and undocumented students, less than 70 percent of respondents described the campus as welcoming.
- About half of employees and nearly 60 percent of students who responded felt WMU promotes racial/cultural interaction between diverse groups.
- Safety on campus was a strength among the employees and students who completed the survey; 86 percent of employees reported they feel safe on campus, as did 76 percent of students. ("Update" 2021)

Building on the affirmed core values of diversity and inclusion, while acknowledging equity gaps in which populations are welcomed more than others, WAC specialists must connect their work to institutional core values and initiatives to articulate the relevance of our work in higher education. In the next chapter, I outline relationships between relevance and the advocacy of resources to support WAC and diversity and inclusion work.

CONCLUSION

While the work done with respect to WAC and diversity and inclusion is still in the nascent state of institutional change, such work still offers insights on the ways in which WPAs might become empowered to connect diversity and inclusion with WAC beyond campus writing programs and departments. This work also expands WAC efforts to reach academic deans and senior leadership. Finally, this work can, nonetheless, become the future of how writing studies considers contributions to WAC scholarship.

4

TOWARD AN INSTITUTIONAL TRANSFORMATION OF WAC
A View Forward Despite Shrinking Operating Budgets

Consider the invitation our students receive when they apply for admission to the institutions where we teach. Instead of considering the admissions team as the gatekeepers for postsecondary entrance and instead of considering our introductory writing courses as gatekeepers to advanced writing courses, however, let's position students as the gatekeepers to higher education enrollment. Let's consider the following facts: (1) There are fewer high school graduates, and the rate of high school graduation continues to decline (Nadworny 2019); (2) postsecondary enrollment has continued to decline since 2011 (Nadworny 2019; Nietzel 2019); (3) in 2017–2018, whites comprised the minority of college enrollment for the first time; and (4) despite the fact that the pool of Black and Latinx 18-year-olds in the US is not shrinking at the same rate as the pool of white 18-year-olds, especially in regions like the Midwest and Northeast, Black enrollment has fallen sharply since 2017 (Miller 2020). Given these sobering statistics, students are now making choices about whether or not they want to enroll in a postsecondary institution, making competition among postsecondary institutions keen with more pressure being put on chief marketing and recruitment/ enrollment officers to sell the optimal college experience to prospective students.

                                                            2022 Call for Proposals

I begin this chapter with an excerpt from the 2022 CCCC Convention Call for Proposals that I composed for the organization as the 2022 Program Chair. I start here as I write this final chapter while still dealing with the direct and residual effects of the COVID-19 pandemic. The statistics shared from the excerpt above were sobering before the pandemic; now, however, these facts have been accelerated by it. For instance, undergraduate enrollment has fallen 6.5 percent since 2019 (Whitford 2021). Additionally, many freshmen who decided not

https://doi.org/10.7330/9781646424542.c004

to enroll during the pandemic have yet to return to school. Moreover, "declines among some public institutions may not be due strictly to the pandemic, so it's unlikely they would reverse now. Many public institutions are chronically underfunded and unable to serve as many students as they would like" (Whitford 2021).

So what does this mean for those of us who teach writing, those of us who advocate for WAC resources, and those of us who advocate for teaching and learning centers? The short answer reveals that institutions, especially public institutions with declining enrollments, perhaps do not have the funds or resources to fund all or even some of these resources sufficiently. It means that administrators will have to make tough decisions about which priorities they are able to support, which priorities are valuable but cannot be supported right now, and which priorities simply aren't the institution's priorities. It means nimbleness and flexibility through collaborative partnerships and innovations will be key to how institutions survive during and after the pandemic.

In the CCCC 2022 Call for Proposals, I also encouraged the discipline to make connections to postsecondary writing instruction and diversity and inclusion work, especially in an area of tight budget and resources, noting:

> It is clear that given the shifting demographics of college students who enroll in higher education, we can no longer think about diversity and inclusion as abstract concepts or as buzzwords strategically placed in writing program descriptions or on university webpages. Nor can we rely only on the language of our CCCC mission statement, particularly its first sentence that marks CCCC as "committed to supporting the agency, power, and potential of diverse communicators inside and outside of postsecondary classrooms." (CCCC 2021)

In essence, this call asks us to consider the promises associated with educating students in the pursuit of social justice and the perils of not doing so. This question runs deeply for me, when looking at WMU especially. While I provided discussion and analysis of revising a general education curriculum to enhance writing and diversity and inclusion outcomes, the call is notable for data it references on the enrollment and retention gaps for Black students, especially Black male students. Within the past year (2020–2021), the institution has lost 20 percent of its Black student population ("Enrollment Dashboard" 2021, https://wmich.edu/institu tionalresearch/reportsanddashboards/enrollment). For us, the perils of not recruiting and retaining Black student populations have equated to overall declining enrollments for the institutions and budget and staff reductions due to lack of enrollment revenue. Given this, how do we advocate for essential professional development built around writing, diversity, and inclusion, and how might these efforts support challenges with declining enrollments?

In the previous chapters of this book, I identified the various ways that training in writing studies is transferable to leadership positions beyond writing programs, particularly to forward both the work of diversity and inclusion and WAC outreach. In this chapter, I would like to discuss more directly how to make the case for WAC and faculty development resources to administrators, given declining enrollments and shrinking budgets.

In 2019, two months into my tenure as an associate dean, I had to deal with an unexpected and unavoidable absence of the dean of my unit. As a result, I was instantly required to make budgetary and fiduciary decisions on behalf of the honors college. While I had some experience with understanding budgets in my position at OFD, I did not receive this experience when I was WPA. All operating budgets within the English department were managed by the department chair. Thus, the learning curve for managing operating budgets in higher education was one of the steepest for me in learning my role as associate dean. Now, as a department chair, a significant amount of my time is spent with fiduciary responsibility and the management of funds, endowments, and other resources. Having been on both sides of the table, one advocating for more resources and one making decisions given a lack of resources, I would like to conclude by providing some guidance for how we make the case for faculty development and WAC work.

My experience with operating budgets allowed for a more feasible transition into my now role as department chair of an interdisciplinary unit, one that is required to generate revenue for the College of Arts and Sciences. Similarly to WMUx and OFD, the previous unit in the honors college was a service unit without revenue-generating responsibilities. Later in this chapter, I will go into more detail about the relationships between revenue-generating and service units and their effects on how we make the case for funding WAC initiatives, given institutional shrinking budgets.

Now that I have gained experience with managing and overseeing department- and college-level operating budgets, I have come to understand that the feasibility of establishing a WAC stand-alone program as one within a larger unit like a teaching and learning center is very closely tied to two main factors: the types of support that state-funded institutions receive and the budget model for distributing funding at a specific institution. Perhaps it was through my former experience as acting dean that I had come to understand the strategic benefits for WAC and faculty development centers to work collaboratively and not in isolation: in an era of declining enrollments at many institutions across Michigan, institutions also forced to rely less and less on state appropriation to support its work simply do not have enough resources to fund many stand-alone units, especially those that are not perceived as interdisciplinary or campus-wide. As a result, strategies are needed to prepare WAC specialists on how to carry the work of WAC out at an institution without the funding to support its work as a distinct unit. In the meantime, the work of writing must carry on to support our students.

In the sections that follow, I will identify a few threats and opportunities to WAC programs and ways that strategic campus-wide collaborations between faculty development and WAC can combat vulnerable units in danger of being eliminated. In order to understand these threats and opportunities, however, I first discuss the institutional context for how institutions generate revenue to support such programs and how this context limits one's ability to develop a stand-alone program. Next, I discuss how the specific budgetary model for resource distribution on which an institution relies to run programs contributes to a unit's vulnerability. Given budgetary challenges to units that are small or identified as service and non-revenue-generating, I also describe a few strategies on how we might elevate WAC intellect through faculty development to reach a larger institutional scale through the process of centralization, a process that allows for specific subvention to university service units. Finally, diversity, as I have argued throughout this book, can be leveraged as an opportunity to elevate both WAC and faculty development intellectual work.

CHALLENGES TO DIVERSIFYING INSTITUTIONAL REVENUE: THREATS TO STAND-ALONE UNITS

The state-funded institutions that face declining enrollment trends are the most vulnerable to the use of budgetary cuts to balance university budgets. Often when we talk about public campaigns and their assaults on higher education, we frame these conversations within the context of federal funding from a national perspective. There isn't a shortage of articles in the *Chronicle of Higher Education* ruing negative perceptions of the value of a higher education degree in the United States. In a 2019 *Chronicle of Higher Education* article, for example, Karin Fischer laments:

American colleges have weathered public criticism before, of course—from the campus unrest of the 1960s to the more-recent student-debt crisis—but they now face new levels of skepticism and mistrust. A substantial swath of voters, including half of Democrats and three-quarters of Republicans, think higher education is going in the wrong direction, and polls show public confidence falling. Americans worry that college costs too much, wonder what students are learning, and question the value of a degree. (2019, par. 5)

The problem with focusing so much on the national crisis in higher education is that it often ignores the complexities of state budgets to higher education, complexities that more directly impact an institution's ability to have the appropriate resources to implement a quality education. For institutions like WMU, it is the downward trends in state appropriations and the decline in high school graduates across the state of Michigan, where we do most of our recruiting for enrollment, that have impacted the amount of funding we are able to generate to deliver key services. By 2023, the number of students who graduate high school from Michigan will decline by 9 percent (NCES 2016). In the state of Michigan, "from FY 2000–01 to FY 2013–14, state appropriations to public universities for operating costs have been reduced by about 30% on a per-student basis, while the average tuition and fee rate charged to an in-state undergraduate student has increased by about 150%" (Jen 2013). Moreover, specifically at WMU, state appropriations between 2001 and 2013 have declined 11.3 percent (32). State-funded institutions like WMU have relied on increases in tuition to compensate for some of the lack of state support and have increased tuition more than 192 percent over this time period; however, state-funded institutions also have a cap on the percentage of tuition increases. Such institutions are also facing trends in declining enrollment that do not offset decreases in state funding. Surviving these budgetary challenges often means the elimination of programs, cuts in programs or units, and the merging of units and programs. It is difficult for writing specialists to make the case for developing a new unit or program when there are no increases in enrollment to support evidence of need. It is also difficult to make the case for a new unit when other units and institutes are being eliminated or merged.

SHIFTING BUDGET MODELS: THREATS TO STAND-ALONE UNITS

While the case can be made that declining state appropriations for state-funded schools is indeed a national trend, a more local and micro look at examining operating budget expenses requires institutions to think more carefully about the relationships between their operational budgets and institutional priorities. Given budgetary challenges, it may not be possible for state-funded institutions who must now rely dispro- portionately on tuition-generated revenue to support programs that do not generate revenue themselves. Thus, understanding the feasibility of developing a stand-alone unit requires a precise understanding of the institution's unique budget model. At WMU, we are in the process of shifting from an incremental budget model, "a top-down approach to budget development, with the view that the current budget is the 'base to which increments (salary and inflation adjustments, new faculty posi- tions and so on) are added to build next year's budget" (Curry, Laws, and Strauss 2013, 13–14), to a version of a responsible-centered budget model (RCM), where incentives are provided to academic units "for all entrepreneurial activities" to keep the revenue they generate to support their operational costs and initiatives (16). With RCMs, service units that do not generate revenue are supported by taxing the revenue- generating units that benefit from their services. In this case, an RCM "utilizes 'subvention' to achieve a balance between local optimization and investment in the best interest of the university as a whole" (17). With the RCM model, academic units act as their own centers, some- thing that contrasts with the incremental budget model, where this is one central office from which budget allocations flow.

Both models pose challenges to making the case for WAC stand-alone units; faculty development centers are also vulnerable, though I would argue they are more vulnerable under an RCM than they are under an incremental or centralized model. With an incremental model, campus- wide centers that cross disciplines and are not perceived as aligning too heavily with one discipline, such as teaching and learning centers, are often understood as adding value to the work of the university. They are often well known and understood as the places where faculty receive professional development and support. Institutions understand inher- ently that they must value centers for teaching and learning, activities central to the mission of the university. They also are less vulnerable to budgetary scrutiny, because in a centralized budget model it remains unclear what the true costs are associated with operating these service units. Because of their campus-wide reach, universities often commit to funding them even if their units do undergo incremental cuts over the years. In contrast, because institutions often associate WAC work with English specialists, these units often do not have the expanded reach of larger teaching and learning centers. As a result, institutions often determine that WAC stand-alone units are too small to fund centrally and often house WAC work within English departments or, even if stand-alone units, as smaller programs that are supported by grant funding or temporary funding.

Both faculty development and WAC programs are vulnerable under an RCM model, however, because they do not generate revenue unless they are awarded external grant funding or donations. With state institutions, the majority of the revenue is generated through tuition, and it is rare that service units that support faculty and teaching will include courses for which students pay tuition, and even in some instances where specialized WAC programs house specific courses, these courses typically have smaller class sizes and are fewer in number, so they do not generate enough tuition revenue to cover their operating expenses. As a result, units such as these must rely on the subvention rules that institutions put in place. In order to rely on these subventions, however, the university has to identify the service unit as a priority, one critical to the work of the whole institution. And the academic units that pay a tax for these subunits will be sure to scrutinize carefully the degree to which faculty in their units recognize and utilize value in the services that service units offer. Larger units are less vulnerable to this scrutiny. While I have made the case that WAC work is institutional work in its scope, its relatively small program size, staff personnel, and support make it vulnerable to scrutiny regarding whether it is indeed an institutional priority.

Put more simply, disciplinary arguments, particularly often associated with making the case for WAC stand-alone units, typically do not sway college-level administrators. As James E. Porter and colleagues (2000) reminded us two decades ago, "Attacking institutional problems only at a global and disciplinary level doesn't work because institutions to too easily ignore global arguments for local reasons (such as lack of available faculty). Universities are not likely to be swayed by particular fields and disciplines. Idealized wish lists are far using 'budgetary realities' as a rationale" (616). Such is clearly the case at WMU. Like the authors, I also continue to be concerned "when global critiques exist only in the form of ideal cases or statements, which all too often bracket off discussions of materiality and economic constraints in favor of working out the best case scenario—which, all too often, does not come to pass" (615). In other words, much of the intellectual work needed to make the case for a WAC presence on college campuses focuses on ideal scenarios and not on what writing specialists can do in the meantime absent a formal programmatic presence given the local economic realities of many institutions. Thus, in the next section, I begin to make the case for opportunities in the meantime.

Some may argue that regardless of the model (RCM, incremental, etc.), most institutions set aside funds to support units that cannot generate their own revenues, like the university libraries, the president's office, or the provost's office, to name a few. As previously mentioned, subvention with an RCM enables this support by subventing or taxing the responsibility units. For those who do not have RCM models, many institutions use an "initiative-based budget," which is "an organised way of creating a pool of money for funding new initiatives than a comprehensive budget system" (Linn 2007, 26). One of the key features of initiative-based funding is that it entails "identifying resources, that will be returned to central administration redistribution in support of the priorities agreed upon during the institution's planning process. In theory, the resources offered up by the units will be for lower-priority or unproductive activities" (Goldstein 2005, 174). The challenge to this model is that it is not a system that one can rely on permanently, especially when enrollment declines (Zierdt 2009, 348; Goldstein 2005, 175; Linn 2007, 26). Put simply, initiative-based funding is often for a limited time, while the work of WAC and faculty development requires permanent support.

STRATEGIC RESOURCE MANAGEMENT: OPPORTUNITIES FOR WAC PROGRAM COLLABORATION

The strategic resource management model at WMU was created by stakeholders and leaders. This model seeks to balance decentralized subvention with responsibility units. At the time at WMU, the budget protocol for a WAC director was submitted initially under an incremental budget model that would report to OFD. In the end, OFD was awarded a faculty fellow who receives a one-course buyout per semester in addition to summer compensation to develop WAC workshops and professional development resources. One might wonder how, if an institution does not prioritize funding a WAC program or WAC director under a centralized model such as an incrementally based one, will WAC—and even faculty development—programs survive under an RCM where cost centers are rewarded for their ability to generate revenue? The answer might lie in a model that balances many of the principles that incentivize revenue generation with strategizing an institution's priorities through centralized funding. WMU's move to a strategic resource management model offers a budget model that reflects a variation of RCM while also identifying specific priorities that will be funded through centralized funds. For OFD work in relation to the new budget model, it functions as a service unit, meaning that it relies on institutional support of priorities since it does not generate its own revenue. This institutional model operates under the following guided principles:

1. **Accountability:** Leaders in each budget unit must ensure that their budget processes and resource allocations align with the strategic resource management guiding principles and the University's strategic plan.

2. **Adaptability:** Budget model should be adaptable to changing circumstances and be regularly reviewed and revised as the University learns more about the process and outcomes.

3. **Balance:** Monitoring the balance between incentives and control provided to colleges and the "common good" of the University community. Both financial and curricular considerations should be used in determining the balance.

4. **Central Funds Investment:** A central pool of funds should be maintained to provide supplemental support for the implementation of University strategic initiatives.

5. **Collaboration:** Budget model should encourage collaboration across the University community.

6. **Communication:** Constant and direct communication should occur to ensure all campus stakeholders are thoroughly informed and on the new budget model elements, issues and processes.

7. **Data:** A robust data environment must be maintained for the new budget model to be implemented, administered and analyzed.

8. **Full Cost:** Full costs (e.g., salaries, supplies, scholarships, debt, utilities) should be aligned with revenue streams where appropriate.

9. **Governance:** The inclusion of shared governance and technical expertise will provide appropriate oversight of the new budget model.

10. **Incentives:** Budget model should provide appropriate and logical budgetary incentives to enhance revenues and to control costs.

11. **Negative Outcomes:** Budget model should anticipate and avoid negative outcomes by providing sufficient funding and agreements to support valued higher cost efforts.

12. **Predictability:** Budget model should have rules that are clear and consistently applied, resulting in predictable outcomes that enable effective planning throughout campus.

13. **Simplicity:** Budget model should be kept simple even though the details of costs and revenues can be complex.

14. **Transparency:** Budget model should be implemented and maintained in a clear, consistent and transparent manner. (WMUSRM 2018)

Principles 3–5 lend themselves to opportunities to make the case for WAC and faculty development collaborations. As previously argued, WAC programs might be perceived as too small in scope (even when they are not) to be identified as priority units. This does not suggest, however, that we cease making the case that writing instruction across disciplines is the responsibility of all who teach and assign writing in our respective fields and, therefore, should be a campus-wide priority. But due to the sheer fact that there is so much institutional variation in where WAC programs are housed, with some in English departments, others freestanding, and others lacking in formal structure (Condon and Ruiz 2012), it is difficult for WAC specialists to make the case for another new program or center, whether under incremental or RCM budget models. That said, SRM creates opportunities for collaborations between faculty development and WAC programs, because (1) the institution is not required to make an immediate decision about funding and subventing a new cost center through centralized funds, (2) the university recognizes efforts to balance revenue with curricular needs since both faculty development and WAC touch faculty and instructors campus-wide, (3) the university sees efforts to collaborate across campus and programs and already has a centralized unit (OFD in this case) to house accountability and foster collaboration and communication, and (4) the disciplinary rationales typically used to make the case for institutional change do not account for local institutional structures and economic conditions. Further, it is easier to justify having a centralized unit of funds to support institutional priorities when a centralized cost center like OFD already exists. The more institution-wide and less disciplinarily tailored our WAC outreach efforts are, the better position we are in to make the case for WAC and faculty development outreach as institutional priorities.

DIVERSITY AND INCLUSION WORK: OPPORTUNITIES FOR WAC WORK THROUGH CENTRALIZATION

In fairness, budgetary survival is not a new concept with respect to WAC programs. Susan McLeod and Margot Soven's (1989) discussion described the challenges for even successful writing programs once grant funding ends (338). David Russell also identifies that many WAC programs failed, "not because they lacked substance, but because they could not overcome the very obstacles which WAC programs are facing today." (1987, 184). More specifically, the organizational structures behind programs that could not survive were limited in their ability to be sustained by cross-institutional partnerships (185). More recently, post-2020 WAC scholarship on funding and sustainability has pointed to similar problems. Chris Anson (2021) notes that models that focus specifically on individuals passionate about teaching writing are difficult to sustain, especially when funding dries out:

This model has effectively served the needs of many campuses, especially because there is something compelling about colleagues who share their inspiration and excitement about teaching with writing. But such programs sustain themselves only because someone is loudly trumpeting their causes: there is nothing particularly "institutional" about the activity. When the grant program dries up or the leader moves on to other pursuits or retires, or the sometimes modest funding for their course release(s) disappears, the effort often shrivels up or goes with them, leaving behind only the fond memories of a once vibrant collective dedicated to curricular and pedagogical change. (6)

It is for this reason that institutional partnerships are so essential for sustaining WAC programs. Individual passion does not translate to subsidies for institutions to invest funding to support non-revenue-generating initiatives.

As previously mentioned, the process of centralization refers to grouping a series of programs and departments under one unit so that operations, practices, and systems are streamlined and consistent. Centralization is key in many ways to ensuring that institutions have fulfilled their missions. As Zierdt (2009) suggests, "the tax proceeds are combined with other central revenues to create a subvention pool that funds centers that are unable to generate sufficient revenues to finance their operations" (349). While centralization often seems to conflict with RCM, which incentivizes decentralized responsibility units with generating their own revenue, not every unit in a university can be decentralized, with the university library system being one of many examples that illustrate this since it cannot generate its own revenue. Zeirdt also acknowledges:

> RCB [Responsibility Centered Budget] has also been criticised for the shift of culture that it can create, most notably the concentration on bottom line as opposed to academic quality; the insulation of units providing internal service against utilising central services; and the challenges of collective bargaining decisions, within unionised campuses, across cost centres. (349)

In other words, responsibility units may desire to create their own services with the hope that they won't have to pay the subvention (tax) for the central service. A prime example of this is when responsibility units like academic colleges (e.g., engineering and business) create their own writing and communication centers that focus on writing specifically in their disciplines. These likely compete with the centralized campus writing center that serves the entire institution. Given this, WAC and writing centers are vulnerable to duplications of services by other colleges and units, many of which are staffed by faculty who lack formal training in rhetoric and composition. To combat threats like these, WAC programs and writing centers must form formal partnerships through larger centralized units. For example, the process of subvention, a tax that responsibility units pay to ensure that service units can operate, provides resources for centralized units to operate, like OFD, WMUx, and Merze Tate College, as discussed in the previous chapter.

From a budgetary perspective, WAC specialists can benefit from stronger collaborations with larger locations like teaching and learning centers and university colleges; support and allyship from teaching and learning centers are also often necessary for early phases of WAC development. But larger campus-wide initiatives like those associated with diversity and inclusion are also necessary, and WAC programs often lack the infrastructure or disciplinary expertise to do this work alone in silos. Take, for instance, the lack of diversity training and scholarship in WAC and WPA intellectual work. While recent conversations to consider intersections between race and gender in WPA work are beginning to be recognized (Craig and Perryman-Clark 2011; Craig and Perryman-Clark 2016; Perryman-Clark and Craig 2019), the field has a long way to go to improve diversity and inclusion practices. Moreover, as discussed in chapter 3, WAC's presence with diversity and inclusion also remains underexplored.

When forming diversity partnerships, it is also critical to collaborate with diversity equity and inclusion offices. The "Standards of Professional Practice for Chief Diversity Officers in Higher Education 2.0" by Worthington, Stanley, and Smith (2020) recommends that diversity officers "strive to optimize the balance between centralization and decentralization of efforts to achieve equity, diversity, and inclusion throughout the institution" (3). Challenges to these responsibilities include but are not limited to:

> (a) the organizational structure in the portfolio of the [chief diversity officer] CDO, (b) the allocation of human, fiscal, and physical resources, (c) the optimal degree of centralization versus decentralization of EDI [equity, diversity and inclusion] efforts, (d) the processes of building institutional and organizational capacity, (e) the unique manifestations of institutional change, and (f) the specific focus and metrics related to accountability. (4)

While these standards do consider units that are decentralized, it is important to understand that most diversity and inclusion offices do not have the infrastructure, resources, or staff to collaborate with every standalone unit. Therefore, collaborations with larger centralized units can allow for consistent implementation of DEI initiatives across campuses.

Finally, building partnerships between WAC and diversity and inclusion through teaching and learning centers enables us to connect the work that we do back to university mission and vision statements; mission and vision statements themselves suggest centralized and consistent sets of aspirations, principles, and values. In chapter 6 of *Afrocentric Teacher-Research*, I urged composition instructors to align the CCCC's Students' Right to Their Own Language resolution with institutional "policy and mission statements" (2013, 122). I echo that call with a similar one here for WAC programmatic outreach, but I also extend this call to include the infrastructure already in place with teaching and learning centers, to facilitate ways to enhance such alignment. I now understand that a key component to this alignment is understanding the institution's strategic plan for how an institution's mission and vision become actualized in practice. Drawing from WMU's new strategic plan, launched in fall 2021, the plan seeks to address seven key priorities:

- Academic Excellence
- Diversity, Equity, and Inclusion
- Well-being
- Sustainability
- Research and Innovation
- Internationalization
- Community Building

Also of note is the fact that strategic plans provide connections between institutional resources and priorities. These objectives are not viewed in isolation of the work of diversity and inclusion and academic excellence, which is why campus models like university colleges are needed to ensure that institutions are indeed welcoming to students from historically oppressed populations. Institutional resources are vital to doing the intellectual work of both teaching and learning and diversity and inclusion. The benefit of larger institutional structures, like larger units for instructional design and innovation and university colleges, is that they make subvention of service units more easily identifiable. Given WAC's smaller infrastructure, and the limited scholarship on diversity and inclusion available, WAC is not equipped as a freestanding unit to meet WMU's institutional needs. This is not to suggest that faculty development centers have all of the resources necessary to respond to diversity and inclusion priorities either; however, as discussed in the previous chapter, these centers have historically identified diversity and inclusion programming as an area of need and have worked to develop programming in response to these needs. In this way, they have had a head start on such programming compared to what has been available in WAC professional development. Specifically at WMU, diversity and inclusion as it relates to teaching and learning has been developed in OFD, and such training and development can be helpful for writing specialists on campus, particularly as additional writing educators emerge to build first-year writing, baccalaureate, and essential studies curricula. As both an administrator and a rhetorician, I would argue that it is more expedient to make the case for WAC and diversity and inclusion resources through larger institutional structures designed with centralization in mind. The process of centralization enables more deliberate subvention for service units whose budget models more closely resemble RCMs.

Of WMU's most recent $550 million donation to support diversity and inclusion work, $200 million is allocated to academic affairs to support diversity and inclusion causes that include student scholarship and faculty and staff hires, with the hope of changing demographics of faculty ranks and research (WMU 2021b). The case for hiring WAC faculty cannot be made in isolation of hiring diverse faculty; moreover, a welcoming environment that celebrates diversity in the classroom and within academic ranks is essential. If we put resources into recruiting and retaining faculty, we must indeed allocate resources to supporting their professional development and advancement.

CONCLUSION

This chapter identifies some key threats to WAC programs as stand-alone units. Using the process of centralization, especially as related to institutional budget models, enables us to connect the WAC, faculty development, and diversity and inclusion work with larger missions and initiatives that reflect institutional values. This, then, enables us to align our work with existing strategic plans. Collaborations with centralized units make visible the work that we do when stand-alone programs are threatened by budgetary constraints.

5

NOW WHAT?
Final Strategies of Forming Partnerships

WHERE HAVE WE BEEN?

Perhaps as a field, we've failed to make our own professional practices as inclusive as they should be, so we find ourselves at a moment when we are scrambling to justify our existence and DEI seems the most convenient way to do so. As a clear and direct caution, the concluding remarks I offer here are plain and simple: be real about this work; don't do it simply for financial incentives, professional recognition, or unit survival. Do it because it is the right thing to do, while being strategic about the collaborations you form to make institutional progress and effect change. This change will not happen overnight, no matter how centralized and efficient the infrastructure is and how much money administrative leaders allocate to this work.

We first need to acknowledge the work we have not done for the struggle and how to move forward. For example, in *Black Perspectives in Writing Program Administration,* Collin Lamont Craig and I critiqued documents like the "Framework for Success in Postsecondary Writing" and the *WPA* journal's Assessment Gallery for their omission of contributions by people of color and Black student-writers. Using linguistic diversity and the lack of inclusion as one example, we note that within the framework "language is positioned as an obstacle/liability and not as an asset that can help foster collaborations on linguistic diversity across cultural and verbal contexts" (2019, 106). As such, how can we as WAC and WPA specialists communicate the value of linguistic diversity across disciplines when as a field we have not reconciled internally the ways in which it can be framed with regard to postsecondary success in writing?

Similar arguments were also made in my 2022 CCCC Call: "Given enrollment challenges, as a discipline that is committed to the teaching of postsecondary instruction, we can no longer be exclusive about what writing belongs and which writings belong in our classrooms" (CCCC 2021). The specific conference theme further encouraged the

https://doi.org/10.7330/9781646424542.c005

discipline to consider "the relationship between access, enrollment, and relevance" (CCCC 2021). Promoting access in writing is our vehicle to improving enrollment (both for recruitment and retention). Practicing diversity and inclusion is what provides relevance for what we do as a field and how we contribute to the greater mission of higher education.

While I have acknowledged some groundbreaking works that move the field forward, especially Sheila Carter-Tod and Jennifer Sano-Franchini's (2021) *WPA* special issue on #BlackLivesMatter, as a field we still have a long way to go in adopting inclusive practices in the way that we work with other scholars in our field—let alone at local sites on our college campuses. In this vein, faculty development teaching and learning and even diversity and inclusion offices can provide the professional development necessary to help us understand how we can be more inclusive as colleagues. While working on revisions to this book, a controversial exchange erupted on our field's WPA-L listserv, with one scholar signing their name as "Grand Scholar Wizard," a nod which evokes the rhetorical discourse of the KKK's grand wizard during the reconstruction period of 1865–1869 (Wade 1998). With another instance, also in the now-defunct WPA-L, at least one WPA reader evoked the metaphor of being "lynched" on the listserv because of his views, a metaphor that dismisses the history of Black citizens lynched in the US. But closer to my institutional home and away from the WPA listserv, I recently had to reprimand a colleague for sharing with me that faculty in their unit would lynch them, reminding them of the coded language they used to me as a woman of color. Of lynching, Ersula Ore (2019) reminds us that "the campaign to save face and rescue whiteness through rhetorical frames that deny lynching continues" (6). The use of lynching in such a way reinforces white supremacy; denying its intent as a white supremacist trope further frames the denial of the continued existence of lynching.

Administrative leadership and rising through faculty development ranks cannot protect me from the dangers of white supremacy, with increasingly frequent uses of the *n*-word by faculty, scholars, and professionals on college campuses being yet another example of the impacts of white supremacy in institutional practice. Our field has also had to contend with a speaker's use of the *n*-word in a public conference presentation. Recently, the Black Student Union at WMU also responded to the administration with a complaint about a faculty member's use of the *n*-word in one of their classes. Yet, another example identifies WMU's own women's track coach being fired for his use of the *n*-word (Robinson 2019, par. 5). And with yet another example, when I was dean I was asked to read an essay that uses the *n*-word in a class for another faculty member, because they were not comfortable with saying the word but thought it might be more appropriate for me to say the *n*-word instead. Examples such as these reflect a clear institutional need for faculty development training on diversity and inclusion, training that must include anti-racist training. The work of WAC alone is not enough to respond to the increasing demands of anti-racist professional development as it pertains to teaching and learning activities on college campuses. Clearly, these examples of racism should remind us that if we did in fact have all of the cultural competence necessary to fulfill our roles as WAC specialists within our field, we would not have this many recent occurrences with which the field and our institutions must grapple. To that end, collaboration with units like teaching and learning centers to develop and participate in cultural competence training serves as an opportunity for writing specialists to receive the necessary diversity and inclusion training as it relates to both teaching and learning and workplace practices. In what follows, I review some of the scholarship that bridges WAC and diversity and inclusion and then offer three concrete recommendations to assist with beginning partnerships and collaborations.

The question now to consider is where conversations about diversity do exist in WAC scholarship. Some of these conversations in WAC scholarship pertain to global engagement initiatives. Tiane Donahue's (2008) review essay, "Cautionary Tales: Ideals and Realities in Twenty-First-Century Higher Education," makes the case for aligning WAC programming with globalization efforts to enhance diversity and inclusion, a discussion that often addresses linguistic diversity for writers of world Englishes. Donahue identifies WAC movements in the UK as centered around "meaning-making and identity [as connected to] teaching and learning across the curriculum" and as models for US WAC outreach (545). In her analysis of Mullin's work, Donahue writes the following:

> Mullin recommends four steps for colleagues: use research "to build inter-disciplinary knowledge that informs the teaching of writing locally and globally"; involve colleagues in writing across the curriculum; establish writing centers; and engage the public in changing the understanding of writing as skills (175). Three of these four activities are highly collaborative interdisciplinary intellectual projects, exactly what should give us hope. Unfortunately, the third collection reviewed here shows that this kind of work is not yet fully valued in U.S. institutions. (549–50)

What is significant about Donahue's discussion is the fact that WAC outreach and commitments to global engagement are intellectual concepts that lend themselves to potential collaborations and partnerships; however, such work is not currently valued in twenty-first-century higher education, a claim that is consistent to my previous discussion about WAC outreach and diversity efforts:

> While US higher education institutions are seeing increases in international student populations, and while many institutions (mine, especially) are developing global engagement initiatives, the connections between WAC and global initiatives through world Englishes and languages does not mirror this commitment. In chapter 6 of *Afrocentric Teacher-Research: Rethinking Appropriateness and Inclusion*, I called for stronger aligning of WAC outreach to Language Across the Curriculum (LAC) initiatives to enhance institutional commitments toward diversity and inclusion, noting that such an alignment would bolster the case for students' right to their own language with "movements with which university administrators are more likely familiar" (Perryman-Clark, 2019, 128).

Another contribution to WAC and linguistic diversity alignment includes Terry Myers Zawacki and Michelle Cox's (2014) collection, *WAC and Second Language Writers: Research towards Linguistically and Culturally Inclusive Programs and Practices*. Acknowledging that WAC research and scholarship entered conversations on linguistic diversity and pedagogy late in comparison to most scholarship on second language writers (Cox and Zawacki 2014, 5), Jonathan Hall contends in the collection's foreword the following about WAC pedagogy and linguistic diversity:

> If we are truly to situate ourselves both critically and consciously in a global context and at the same time attend to the intensely local characteristics of a unique campus population, and of the various needs of the individuals within that population, a consciousness of linguistic diversity has to be a factor in all of WAC's administrative and pedagogical decisions; it must be explicitly included, because otherwise we may easily fall back on our unspoken assumptions of monolingualism. (8)

What is critical to emphasize here is the need to attend to both global and local contexts when considering WAC programmatic outreach. Hall also acknowledges that local contexts are critical when developing WAC programs, but since no two programs are the same (6), it is essential to also acknowledge the global roots associated with WAC development that have existed across systems of higher education for decades (6–7). In *Afrocentric Teacher Research*, I have drawn similar parallels between WAC and the Language Across the Curriculum (LAC) movements, with LAC being one of the earliest historical examples of global engagement in relation to professional development in both the military and higher education (120). In addition, an emphasis on global engagement and WAC is essential to fulfill institutional missions of higher education in their commitments to diversity. My own institution, for example, touts global engagement as one of the three pillars of its mission statement. Establishing a WAC program that aligns with the University's mission, then, helps potentially support the institution's commitment to diversity.

As also connected to faculty development, Hall (2014) further asserts that a firm commitment to linguistic diversity extends beyond the traditional faculty development workshop (12). While a starting point, WAC outreach needs to position linguistic diversity as foundational to transforming institutions, a point consistent with those argued in chapter 6 of *Afrocentric Teacher Research*. In chapter 5 of Cox and Zawacki's collection, Kathryn Nielsen (2014) presents findings from her qualitative study on Generation 1.5 students' perceptions of WAC faculty and white native English speakers in the classroom. Nielsen defines Generation 1.5 students as a "diverse range of multilingual, immigrant learners who were born and educated outside the United States and who enter the US educational system while in the process of learning English" (130). She further connects admission of Generation 1.5 students at her institution to increased demands for faculty development support around writing (130), while also acknowledging that her current institution lacks sufficient faculty development support for 1.5 writers (133). Nielsen's findings reveal that while Generation 1.5 students felt that faculty valued "the diversity of thought and experience they brought in the classroom," they still experienced discrimination, often in the form of racial microaggressions (145). Such a finding underscores the important role of faculty development programming in helping faculty identify and overcome the implicit (and explicit) biases they may inflict on students of color, especially students whose first language is other than English. Moreover, while WAC scholarship has just begun to really scratch the surface with regard to linguistic diversity and race (Anson 2012), there is clearly more work needed to help faculty adjust their pedagogies and attitudes about students of color and ESL speakers and writers.

Even more recently, Lucy R. McNair and Leigh Garrison-Fletcher (2022) have addressed the connections between the Language Across the Curriculum movement and WAC, noting that language instruction related to WAC requires a revision of historically color-blind approaches to teaching ESL speakers and writers:

> The British model of LAC is similar to the Writing Across the Curriculum (WAC) movement in the US (Parker, 1985). Both WAC and Writing in the Disciplines (WID) have successfully engaged whole institutions in addressing the challenges of writing and reading. At our institution, many students and faculty have benefited from WAC and WID approaches and

training. However, this training has been largely language-blind, with limited discussion of multilingualism and insights from applied linguistics. (4)

Both authors emphasize the need for broader institutional engagement and collaboration, including interdisciplinary collaborations similar to those discussed in chapter 3 (5). Of these collaborations, the authors note the influence and necessity for faculty development centers, what they refer to as Centers for Teaching and Learning (CTLs). Both describe this collaboration in the following way:

> With the support of a CTL colleague, Leigh developed and co-led a mini-seminar tied to FYS where they initiated a college-wide effort to engage in discussions of language diversity. "Supporting ESL Students in the First Year Seminar" was linked to the faculty seminar and divided into three two-hour sessions with a range of FYS faculty. One result was a "Best Practices" guide for all FYS instructors in approaching multilingual students. Based on this successful effort, the CTL expanded a follow-up seminar to faculty across campus. In three two-hour sessions the participants discussed characteristics of multilingual students, examined some of the academic language used in their disciplines, and discussed best practices for teaching emergent bilingual students and scaffolding discipline-specific language. The consensus from participant feedback was that the seminar was very useful, but only "scratched the surface." (6)

While the connections between interdisciplinary units and faculty development are explicit from this discussion, what is also worth mentioning is the necessity of sustainability. One-off workshops often scratch the surface, an observation consistent with the feedback provided from chapter 3's discussion of the Seminar for Teaching Inclusivity. Sustaining these partnerships, then, requires broader institutional support and resources to support the longevity of programs and initiatives.

DIVERSITY, WAC, AND FACULTY DEVELOPMENT: BUILDING CROSS-INSTITUTIONAL PARTNERSHIPS

Previously in this book, I examined the ways in which WAC scholarship provides opportunities to enhance diversity and inclusion outreach across college campuses. I also pointed to the need for WAC initiatives to include training on linguistic diversity and implicit biases, especially with regard to race. I also referenced Nielsen's admission of the lack of faculty development support to assist with this training. Thus, both WAC and faculty developers point to continued needs and demands for the professional development of diversity. In this section, I will provide opportunities to bridge the divide: Simply put, I will make the case for the ways that faculty development and WAC can partner through diversity and inclusion initiatives, starting with linguistic diversity. In "In Response to Today's 'Felt Need': WAC, Faculty Development, and Second Language Writers," Michelle Cox (2014) indicates the following:

> An important first step for WAC directors interested in creating [linguistic and cultural diversity] programming is to reach out to those directing, staffing, and teaching within programs like these, for several reasons: (1) to learn from information gathered on international and/or multilingual students on your campus; (2) to learn about other faculty development efforts related to L2 students; and (3) to form partnerships for researching L2 writers on campus and offering faculty development. These stakeholders, who share a focus on or interest in multilingual and multicultural students, may be brought together as a working group or taskforce, or, if there isn't the means to organize a formal group, serve individually as potential collaborators whom the WAC director may call upon to co-lead a workshop or present on a particular topic during a workshop. (302–3)

Cox's discussion is perhaps the most specific example of what a WAC initiative designed around faculty development and diversity might look like. Of faculty development activities, Cox identifies "WAC programming, faculty development workshops and faculty consultations" as key locations for providing support and resources to teach second language writers (L2) academic writing across courses and curricula (303). She further identifies faculty development and WAC programming as natural allies for such work (303).

With regard to specific practices, at Bridgewater State University, her home institution at the time, Cox identifies the "First Year Writing Program, the Office of Teaching and Learning, the Office of Institutional Research, the Office of Institutional Diversity, and the Office of Undergraduate Research" as collaborators on faculty development initiatives that pertain to L2 writing pedagogy (302). Programming initially began with understanding faculties' existing attitudes around L2 writers, many of whom still subscribed to a deficit model of language acquisition (303–4). Programming then moved from a deficit model of language, toward a "difference-as-resource" model that sees multilingualism as an addition and not a deficiency (304). Finally, Cox advocates for a "difference-accommodated" model that asks faculty to understand that not only are there cultural differences in the linguistic and rhetorical conventions of other languages but these differences require accommodations in faculty pedagogy. Cox asserts: "While the difference-as-resource stance asks faculty to transform their pedagogy, the difference-accommodated stance asks them to make adjustments to their pedagogy, representing an important incremental step" (305). Cox also acknowledges that her experiences teaching First-Year Writing, working with L2 writers, and serving as WAC director provided her with the advantage for developing such workshops. Such an advantage is consistent with my argument that as WAC and rhetoric and composition specialists, we have the capacity to design faculty development initiatives that transform institutional practices toward diversity and inclusion, a capacity I also argue is not yet fulfilled.

Interestingly, Anson (2021) does make some additional suggestions about the direction of faculty development work around race and WAC, suggesting that faculty development maintain a longer-term role than the traditional WAC workshops typically offered, especially when exploring complex topics such as race, diversity, and inclusion, and suggests the following:

> Racial invisibility in WAC comes not from conscious exclusion. Instead, various historical, political, and disciplinary forces appear to have filtered race and diversity from central consideration in the WAC movement. These forces affect WAC leaders as much as they affect teachers within disciplines. For example, the subject of race is perceived to generate layers of additional complexity over principles, theories, and pedagogies already challenging faculty in various disciplines to interpret and apply to their teaching. Although approaches to deeper, longer-term faculty development in WAC are gaining in popularity, such as learning communities . . . and semester-long seminars . . . , the brief, onetime workshop still enjoys a dominant position as the most common form of WAC delivery. In such contexts, workshop leaders may be reluctant to complicate their agendas by opening discussions of race and diversity before faculty have fully internalized and applied new ideas about how to rethink their roles. (20)

What is critical from Anson's discussion here is a *sustained* effort to include diversity and inclusion as part of the intellectual framework of WAC programs, a sustained effort that extends far beyond the financial sustainability discussed in the previous chapter. Furthermore, the fact that the majority of WAC outreach consists of short-term workshops demonstrates a reluctance to engage complex topics like race and diversity, topics that involve deeper, in-depth, and longer discussions. Anson's discussion particularly resonates for me as a faculty developer, however. While faculty development and teaching and learning centers do offer wide varieties of shorter-term workshops and seminars, such programming does not necessarily comprise the bulk of offerings in comparison to WAC programs. For example, at WMU, workshops only comprise a fraction of our faculty development programming, and most of our programs consist of semester-long series that are offered yearly. Many of our learning communities extend for multiple academic years. The point I emphasize here is that faculty development centers are often equipped to engage complex topics, because such programming doesn't rely mostly on one-time workshops. Thus, faculty development centers provide WAC specialists with increased opportunities to collaborate on topics like race and diversity, especially when considering the ways in which WAC outreach has traditionally overlooked such explorations. In chapter 4, I shared examples of longer-term programming around diversity that were created to sustain diversity and inclusion programming, therefore offering deeper and more in-depth opportunities to identify, explore, and apply diverse teaching and learning practices. Moreover, I emphasize here that writing specialists have much to offer and contribute to such programming.

The work of writing centers in effecting institutional change and progress is not without challenges, however. As Isaacs and Knight (2014) note,

> Writing centers are often perceived as being outside the scope of a WPA's work, even though directing them requires similar expertise . . . At the same time, our research uncovered several centers that suggest the emergence of a new model in which a writing center can serve as the focal point for establishing a culture of writing on campus and in the larger community. Beyond these few highlights, this article provides data on the means by which individualized writing instruction is provided at a range of institutions, thereby presenting a baseline against which future trends can be measured. If WPAs are able to make a case for why particular resources are needed, and for what purpose, they need to have reliable data on existing operations. (37)

Worth also pointing out here are the data described by Isaacs and Knight, which were published long before the COVID-19 pandemic in which colleges now find themselves having to make cuts to critical services to make up for lost revenue while also making cuts due to higher education's enrollment challenges. While Isaacs and Knight also identify some of the strongest units, what they describe as centers for the study or teaching of writing (housing both writing centers and writing programs), as being stand-alone units with their own operating budgets (56), as I described previously in chapter 4 stand-alone units are vulnerable to cuts because administrators often *see* this work as discipline-specific and not within the service of the entire institution.

The work of writing centers is also crucial to how we understand racial diversity and professional development for faculty and administrators. *WPA: Writing Program Administration*'s special issue on #BlackLivesMatter specifically addresses the roles of WPAs and writing centers to transform institutional practices. As editors, Sheila Carter-Tod and Jennifer Sano-Franchini (2021) write, "While programmatic change is important, unless the institutionalized racist practices that are inscribed into curriculum are challenged, sustainable change cannot occur" (17). Specifically, Rebecca Hallman Martini and Travis Webster (2021) in their article in that issue, "Antiracism Across the Curriculum: Practicing an Integrated Approach to WAC and Writing Center Faculty Development," address the role of faculty development in preparing instructors to examine writing assignments, peer-work practices, assessment and evaluation, and language choices made by writers as they incorporate anti-racist teaching (17). In the same issue, Mara Lee Grayson and Siskanna Naynaha's (2021) "Collaboration at the Center: Anti-Racist Writing Program Architecture at California State University Dominguez Hills" addresses how critical it is for institutions to build stronger collaborations between writing programs, writing centers, and other institutional units to effect change and transformation with WAC and anti-racist work.

While racial diversity and linguistic diversity offer starting points, I also believe that WAC specialists can contribute more to shaping diversity conversations beyond these types of diversity. As rhetoricians who think about argument, persuasion, and kairos in nuanced ways, I believe we have much to offer to conversations about culturally diverse content across the curriculum. In chapter 3, I talked about my institution's Teaching Inclusivity Series as an opportunity to contribute to diversity and inclusion programming across the curriculum. While synthesis and examples of contributions were previously discussed, I will simply state here that rhetoric and composition has never shied away from cultural studies or the desire to reimagine composition as a location for cultural rhetorical work (Brodkey 1987; Villanueva and Arola 2003; Powell et al. 2014); however, as I've argued in *Afrocentric Teacher-Research,* our conversations about cross-cultural work have traditionally been limited to work we do within the discipline and within our own writing classrooms. WAC outreach instead provides us with the opportunity to extend our cross-cultural work to a broader university community, and faculty development can serve as a potential designated hub or space for institutions to commit to do such intellectual work. As our Inclusivity Series demonstrated, participants explore wide-ranging diversity concepts included but not limited to racial diversity, LGBTQ+-friendly classroom pedagogies, disability studies and accessibility, and challenging and managing microaggressions on students and colleagues. As WAC specialists who understand the rhetorical nature of argument and discursive practices, I firmly believe we can not only contribute to these conversations but also revise and transform the locations of such practices in our own WAC scholarship and outreach. Given where we have been with WAC scholarship and work, I turn my attention to providing concrete steps forward with creating stronger collaborations with teaching and learning centers in the wake of budgetary constraints.

STEP 1: CONNECT WITH CENTERS FOR TEACHING AND LEARNING CENTERS AND LEARN FROM THEIR CONTRIBUTIONS

The first step is connection before partnerships and partnerships before merging or centralizing. Given the complexity of WAC programmatic models and institutional budget models, the future of WAC development often lies in an institution's ability to foster stronger collaboration. That said, I would be naive not to acknowledge concerns about programmatic merging in challenging budgetary times. For instance, absorbing WAC into larger teaching and learning positions may potentially neglect a focus on writing and WAC professional development altogether. As Ruiz and Condon warn, if "WAC becomes seamlessly incorporated into an institution's approach to teaching and learning—seemingly a positive development—WAC can disappear as an entity, throwing the institution back into some of the problems that gave rise to WAC in the first place" (2012, 379). To be clear, I am not proposing that WAC lack an institutional presence, nor that it simply be included as part of a teaching and learning center. Rather, I posit that WAC should have its own programming, yet could also have an institutional home within a teaching and learning center or university college, especially in times of budgetary cuts. Such a proposition is indeed a start; a possible goal in the future might be for WAC to function as a distinct programmatic unit.

As discussed in the previous chapter, stand-alone units are vulnerable. To make the case for a distinctive unit, one must be able to prove that the program has outgrown its home and that duplicated resource efforts exist minimally if at all. But distinction requires understanding what different components exist between two separate locations. One cannot understand these differences without talking to each other or collaborating when similar goals do exist. Thus, I do believe that the first step to establishing a WAC program begins with forming connections that can lead to collaborations and partnerships with faculty development, to develop a series of Writing to Learn and WAC professional development workshops as discussed previously. Moreover, a known entity like a teaching and learning center gives such development the visibility needed to develop WAC programming when WAC as its own entity bears no institutional presence. As Condon and Ruiz also note:

On one level, WAC must act as a particle. It must exist somewhere; its leadership is crucial, as is the formation and continual reformation of its impacts on curriculum, on student learning. It must have characteristics—and a history. However, if all we can see is WAC's location, then the program remains one of the first two types. It has not yet begun to have the kind of broader institutional impact that results in its being valued by those outside the WAC program and its immediate constituency—its converts. (2012, 380)

The first prototype of WAC programs, as Condon and Ruiz articulate, is foundational, a phase as which I would characterize WMU's current presence. This phase can be typified by the following goals:

- Problem-based statement of purpose;
- Increase writing in curriculum;
- Teaching writing becomes everyone's job;
- Understand difference between learning to write and writing to learn;
- Move beyond inoculation model for learning to write;
- Focus on writing pedagogy;
- Missionary work: gain faculty buy-in for WAC goals;
- Early success based on leadership's energy and charisma; and
- Recruitment of range of faculty to WAC. (Condon and Ruiz 2012, 362–63)

With regard to funding and organizational structure, foundational prototypes are "largely volunteer effort, sometimes with minor reassigned time [and] [d]ependent on good will from umbrella (provost, dean, etc.)" (362). These prototypes also adopt a faculty development model that includes a group of individuals who collaborate (362).

The second phase of prototype bears some similarities to the first in that programmatic development is in the early stages; however, there are key differences. First, the goals: while relying on a faculty development model for vision, there is a concerted and exclusive focus on WAC needs. For funding, the program has its own operating budget, space, staffing, and distinct location. With regard to organizational structure, the second prototype includes the following characteristics:

- Basic administrative existence or implementation;
- Identity of its own, differentiated from general education or other allies;
- People with WAC mapped into workloads;
- Cohort of supporters or stakeholders develops (usual suspects);
- Interdisciplinary policy committee emerges, preferably tied to faculty governance structures;

- Outcomes identified in participatory process;
- WAC scholarship recognized as valuable within institution;
- Incremental improvement, guided by careful processes for change;
- Recruitment expands to include faculty from whole curriculum; and
- Key players/founders/vision people can hand off pieces of program or whole program to others. (362)

The second prototype was clearly a next logical step for WAC development at WMU, where the institution understood that cuts to enrollment and revenue, as driven by the 2020 COVID-19 pandemic, would be needed to sustain the institution while providing the resources students and faculty need. To be clear, I am in no way suggesting that the process of centralization enables institutions to have all the resources they need. But it does provide a hub and template for problem-solving and collaboration, when the institution can no longer resource individual units that may or may not duplicate resources.

STEP TWO: IDENTIFY KEY INITIATIVES ON CAMPUS THROUGH CURRICULUM AND INITIATIVES FOR PARTNERSHIP

While initiative-based funding is not a permanent solution, it does begin the conversation, and once formal partnerships are formed, collaborators can begin with seed money and take advantage of presidential-level or provost-level strategic initiatives to begin critical WAC and faculty development work, especially with respect to diversity and inclusion. Campuses collaborate because they see a particular need or problem the institution needs to solve. In our case, general education was a thirty-five-year-plus problem that the institution had yet to solve. Critical in forming stronger partnerships between faculty development and WAC was the institutional need for general education reform. The fact that WMU had first undergone general education revision and has continued to collaborate with faculty development on WAC initiatives through WMU suggests progress forward. While I have referenced previous scholarship in this book about developing WAC programs (McLeod and Soven), and while much of our WAC scholarship asserts the distinctness and expertise necessary for WAC specialists, only a limited amount of scholarship has paid attention to the budgetary realities facing institutions. Moreover, such limited scholarship has identified the ways in which we might leverage faculty development and teaching and learning centers as allies, with the goal of developing formal WAC programs.

While considering key initiatives for curriculum reform and partnerships, don't forget that diversity, equity, and inclusion must play a critical role in every curricular initiative and reform effort. Embedding diversity and inclusion is essential in curriculum: it affirms and acknowledges the shifting demographics in the US, where students of color will form the campus majority, because it helps us to see clearly the alignment between institutional missions and values, and because it's the precise thing writing scholars should prioritize when thinking about the future of WAC work and writing program administration. WMU's work with general education allows us to see the connections between diversity and inclusion learning outcomes, what students identify as having been learned, and the skills, knowledge, and values that students bring from the writing they do in higher education.

OFD's Seminar in Teaching Inclusivity also helps us understand how forming partnerships is key to solving long-term institutional problems. Both faculty development for writing instruction, and the lack of diversity and inclusion resources for faculty and students were long-standing problems that could not be addressed by a single office or stand-alone unit. It wasn't until we were able to connect multiple units with each other through the Seminar of Teaching Inclusivity that we were able to see the formal partnerships we could build with each other in order to make progress. While this event noted institutional sites for collaboration, it responded to unaddressed, wide-ranging institutional problems. While the institution still needs additional work to address these problems, it offers a starting point that aids WAC and writing specialists with moving forward.

STEP 3: UNDERSTAND THE BUDGET CONSTRAINTS AT WORK AND PREPARE TO WORK WITHIN THEM

Using initiative-based funding is only a starting point. Beyond that, once the partnerships, collaborations, and results have matured, justification of permanence is needed. But be realistic: regardless of quality and productivity, enrollment challenges will often prevent administrators from establishing stand-alone units, especially for institutions where stand-alone WAC programs do not exist. For institutions with long-standing stand-alone programs, budgetary justification will still be needed, so it's indeed necessary to be proactive about justification. When institutions have budgetary constraints, they are less likely to build, maintain, or support stand-alone units that are perceived as not aligning more broadly with the mission of the institution. I recognize, though, that leveraging the process of centralization is not popular, especially for a field that has long argued for its own autonomy. The future of writing studies, however, challenges us to move in a different direction, one that aligns more closely with the realities of higher education and shifting enrollment demographics.

As Condon and Ruiz also describe, the most established WAC prototypes are those which are institutional agents (2012, prototype 4). These programs enable WAC to drive institutional change, contain permanent institutional funding, and maintain an "institutional identity congruent with activities . . . independent of the umbrella (provost or dean's office, etc.)" (2012, 362). Establishing WAC as an institutional agent requires both an established record of effort and time on college campuses and current budget models, and financial pressures make the feasibility of establishing a WAC program as an institutional agent a challenging one, even at large regional public research universities like WMU. In the meantime, WPAs and WAC specialists must be equipped with allies and units with which they can collaborate, ones that potentially have more developed infrastructures. WAC specialists must understand ways to strategize collaborations across units to pool resources together when funding is limited.

The threat to stand-alone writing programs, juxtaposing autonomy with smaller budgets, is not a new one. In "A Rose by Every Other Name: The Excellent Problem of Independent Writing Programs," Wendy Bishop (2002) argued:

> Administrator/faculty also receives a greater degree of (or complete) budgetary autonomy, although some of these programs experienced bait and switch along the lines of "Yes, you have autonomy, but your program is so small and new and unknown you only have this much (i.e., not much) of a budget." (239)

Such a key concern is a critical one, especially in a post-2020 era characterized by COVID and shrinking higher education. Also critical and worth mentioning here is the emphasis on "so small and new and unknown" (239). This is where the previous discussion offered in step two becomes essential: leveraging our expertise with writing and diversity and inclusion enables us to connect with larger and better-known units to partner on key strategic initiatives that enhance the university's mission and values in the pursuit of academic excellence and inclusivity.

Rhetorically speaking, institutions understand that to thrive they must value diversity and inclusion. More specifically, institutions that face enrollment challenges also understand how critical it is that they recruit and retain a diverse student population. Efforts that enhance centralization, like connecting or merging writing centers with a university college, allow us to leverage knowledge, expertise, and contribution with common institutional challenges like student enrollment and retention. Retention efforts require appropriate professional development so faculty are equipped to meet diverse learners' needs in the curricula they design. WAC specialists can contribute tremendous knowledge pertaining to how we teach diverse writers in our classroom. Similarly, WAC specialists can learn a great deal about how, broadly speaking, pedagogical practices like those connecting to ADA compliance, preferred pronouns, and group assignments can be more inclusive and free of cultural bias. As we face challenges questioning the value of higher education and its return on a student's investment, it behooves us to be strategic in how we collaborate with each other across units and to utilize our resources wisely. The work of writing never ends; stakeholders and allyship cross multiple units across college campuses. In short, collaborations between faculty development and WAC to foster diversity and inclusion initiatives offer WAC specialists the opportunity to elevate the case for writing instructional support and resources on college campuses.

More specifically, when thinking about budgetary constraints, we must leverage our partnerships with and within centralized units so we can argue for subvention. Administrators are more likely to subvent a service unit that they see as vital to the institution's existence. As Massy (1996) notes, "enrollment shortfalls produce budget shortfalls, immediately and decisively, the only appeal route being through the difficult subvention route" (34). The list of units that don't generate a larger, market-based revenue, including those units that require smaller enrollments to maintain quality and solid faculty-to-student ratios (e.g., music schools), as well as those that generate no revenue at all because they aren't a market-based generating source, will continue to grow, and more competition and justification of subventions will continue. It will become essential for largely subvented units like university colleges and teaching and learning centers to justify their existence with decreasing room for even smaller units to rely on getting their piece of the subvention as a stand-alone unit. Teaching and learning centers become vital, because with reducing resources, faculty must push administrators to offer the resources they need to teach, recruit students to programs, and retain students, especially under an RCM model. University colleges are essential for subvention, because they offer the support services and programs also needed to recruit and retain students. Diversity and inclusion expertise is also critical to recruitment and retention. In an environment where enrollment drives every conversation we have about students, we also need to demonstrate how faculty development through diversity and inclusion initiatives supports this.

CONCLUSION

In short, what I essentially argue in this book and in this chapter is that faculty development centers should become essential centralized locations for institutions in the nascent phases of WAC programmatic development. Both audiences benefit tremendously from the contributions each can make to enhance teaching and learning initiatives across college campuses. Chapter 2 demonstrated the ways in which coming together to solve a long-standing problem elevated institutional conversations about WAC. Chapter 3 showed how WAC specialists can leverage expertise on writing to form partnerships with teaching and learning centers, especially as connected to diversity and inclusion through the process of centralization. Chapter 4 showed how to work within existing budget constraints while leveraging contributions and partnerships to enhance larger centralized units. Finally, this chapter offers three concrete recommendations for getting started with WAC and faculty development coalition-building, regardless of budget model, existing program status, or stand-alone unit status. It is my hope that readers will understand the larger administrative budgetary constraints and decision-making processes that impact and shape the work we do within the field, especially as connected to WAC, faculty development, and diversity and inclusion.

WORKS CITED

"About." 2021. Western Michigan University, 3 Nov. 2021, https://wmich.edu/strategic/about.

"About Merze Tate College." Western Michigan University, 21 Jan. 2022, https://wmich.edu/merzetate/about.

Ad Hoc Committee on General Education. 2016. *General Education Self-Study February 15, 2016.*

Adler-Kassner, Linda, and John Majewski. 2016. "Extending the Invitation: Threshold Concepts, Professional Development, and Outreach." In Adler-Kassner and Wardle, 253–301.

Adler-Kassner, Linda, and Elizabeth Wardle, eds. 2016. *Naming What We Know: Threshold Concepts of Writing Studies.* Logan: Utah State University Press.

Anson, Chris M. 2012. "Black Holes: Writing Across the Curriculum, Assessment, and the Gravitational Invisibility of Race." In *Race and Writing Assessment,* edited by Asao B. Inoue and Mya Poe, 15–28. New York: Peter Lang.

Anson, Chris M. 2021. "Introduction. WEC and the Strength of the Commons." In *Writing-Enriched Curricula: Models of Faculty-Driven and Departmental Transformation,* edited by Chris M. Anson and Pamela Flash, 3–14. Fort Collins, CO: The WAC Clearinghouse.

Artze-Vega, Isis, Melody Bowdon, Kimberly Emmons, Michele Eodice, Susan K. Hess, Claire Coleman Lamonica, and Gerald Nelms. 2013. "Privileging Pedagogy: Composition, Rhetoric, and Faculty Development." *College Composition and Communication* 65 (1): 162–84.

Bazerman, Charles. 1994. "Systems of Genre and the Enactment of Social Intentions." In *Genre and the New Rhetoric,* edited by Aviva Freedman and Peter Medway, 79–101. New York: Taylor Francis.

Beach, Andrea L., Mary Deane Sorcinelli, Ann E. Austin, and Jaclyn K. Rivard. 2016. *Faculty Development in the Age of Evidence: Current Practices, Future Imperatives.* Herndon, VA: Stylus Publishing.

Bergmann, Linda S. 2008 "Writing Centers and Cross-Curricular Literacy Programs as Models for Faculty Development." *Pedagogy: Critical Approaches to Teaching Literature, Language, Composition, and Culture* 8 (3): 523–36.

Bishop, Wendy. 2002. "A Rose by Every Other Name: The Excellent Problem of Independent Writing Programs." In *A Field of Dreams: Independent Writing Programs and the Future of Composition Studies,* edited by Peggy O'Neill, Angela Cro, and Larry W. Burton, 233–46. Logan: Utah State University Press.

Borboa-Peterson, Stacey, C. Casey Ozaki, and Anne Kelsch. 2021. "Adoption of a Cross-Campus Community of Practice for the Implementation of Equity-Focused Faculty Development." In *Teaching and Learning for Social Justice and Equity in Higher Education,* edited by Laura Parsons and Casey Ozaki, 179–200. New York: Palgrave Macmillan.

Bray, M. 1999. "Control of Education: Issues and Tensions in Centralization and Decentralization." In *Comparative Education,* edited by R. F. Arnove and C. A. Torres, 207–32. Lanham, MD: Rowman & Littlefield.

Brodkey, Linda. 1987. *Academic Writing as Social Practice.* Philadelphia, PA: Temple University Press.

https://doi.org/10.7330/9781646424542.c006

Brodkey, Linda. 1996. *Writing Permitted in Designated Areas Only*. Minneapolis: University of Minnesota Press.

Burnstad, Helen, and Cynthia J. Hoss. 2010. "Faculty Development in the Context of Community College." In Gillespie and Robertson, 309–26.

Camblin, Lanthan D., Jr. and Joseph A. Steger. 2000. "Rethinking Faculty Development." *Higher Education* 39 (1): 1–18.

Carter-Tod, Sheila, and Jennifer Sano-Franchini. 2021. "Introduction: Black Lives Matter and Anti-Racist Projects in Writing Program Administration." *Writing Program Administration* 44 (3): 12–22.

Condon, William, Ellen R. Iverson, Cathryn A. Manduca, Carol Rutz, and Gudrun Willett. 2016. *Faculty Development and Student Learning: Assessing the Connections*. Bloomington: Indiana University Press.

Condon, William, and Carol Ruiz. 2012. "A Taxonomy of Writing Across the Curriculum Programs: Evolving to Serve Broader Agendas." *College Composition and Communication* 64 (2): 357–82.

Conference on College Composition and Communication (CCCC). 2015. "Principles for the Postsecondary Teaching of Writing." Accessed 1 Nov. 2017. http://cccc.ncte.org/cccc/resources/positions/postsecondarywriting.

Conference on College Composition and Communication (CCCC). 2021. "2022 Call for Proposals." December 20, 2021. https://cccc.ncte.org/cccc/call-2022.

Cook, Constance Ewing, and Michele Marincovich. 2010. "Effective Practices at Research Universities: The Productive Pairing of Research and Teaching." In Gillespie and Robertson, 277–92.

Cox, Michelle. 2014. "In Response to Today's 'Felt Need': WAC, Faculty Development, and Second Language Writers." In Zawacki and Cox, 299–326.

Craig, Collin Lamont, and Staci M. Perryman-Clark. 2011. "Troubling the Boundaries: (De)constructing WPA Identities at the Intersections of Race and Gender." *WPA: Writing Program Administration* 34 (2): 37–58.

Craig, Collin Lamont, and Staci M. Perryman-Clark. 2016. "Troubling the Boundaries Revisited: Moving Towards Change as Things Stay the Same." *WPA: Writing Program Administration* 39 (2): 20–26.

Curry, John, Andrew L. Laws, and Jon C. Strauss. 2013. *Responsibility Center Management: A Guide to Balancing Academic Entrepreneurship and Fiscal Responsibility*, 2nd ed. Washington, DC: National Association of College and University Business Officers.

Donahue, Tiane. 2008. "Cautionary Tales: Ideals and Realities in Twenty-First-Century Higher Education." *Pedagogy: Critical Approaches to Teaching Literature, Language, Composition, and Culture* 8 (2): 537–53.

"Elementary and Secondary Enrollment." Coe—Public School enrollment. Accessed April 8, 2022. https://nces.ed.gov/programs/coe/indicator_cga.asp.

"Enrollment." Western Michigan University. Accessed April 8, 2022. https://wmich.edu/institutionalresearch/interactivedashboards/enrollment/data.

Faculty Senate. https://wmich.edu/sites/default/files/attachments/u370/2016/gened selfstudy.2-16-16.pdf.

Fischer, Karin. 2019. "It's a New Assault on the University." *Chronicle of Higher Education*, February 27, 2019. Accessed April 5, 2022. https://www.chronicle.com/article/its-a-new -assault-on-the-university/.

"Framework for Success in Postsecondary Writing—CWPA." 2011. Council of Writing Program Administrators. Accessed April 8, 2022. http://wpacouncil.org/aws/CWPA /asset_manager/get_file/350201?ver=2975.

French, Ron. 2021. "Michigan College Enrollment Dropped amid COVID, Group Urges State to Step In." *Bridge Michigan*, August 20, 2021. Accessed April 5, 2022. https://www .bridgemi.com/talent-education/michigan-college-enrollment-dropped-amid-covid -group-urges-state-step.

Gaff, Jerry, and Ronald D. Simpson. 1994. "Faculty Development in the United States." *Innovative Higher Education* 18 (3): 167–76.

Gillespie, Kay J., and Douglas L. Robertson, eds. 2010. *A Guide to Faculty Development.* Hoboken, NJ: John Wiley & Sons.

Goldstein, Larry. 2005. *College and University Budgeting: An Introduction for Faculty and Academic Administrators.* Washington, DC: NACUBO.

Graham, Joan. 2000. "Writing Components, Writing Adjuncts, Writing Links." In McLeod and Soven, 63–77.

Grayson, Mara Lee, and Siskanna Naynaha. 2021. "Collaboration at the Center: Anti-racist Writing Program Architecture at California State University Dominguez Hills." *Writing Program Administration* 44 (3): 169–76.

Hall, Jonathan. 2014. "Foreword: Multilinguality Across the Curriculum." In Zawacki and Cox, 5–144.

Harper, Rowena, and Karen Orr Vered. 2017. "Developing Communication as a Graduate Outcome: Using 'Writing Across the Curriculum' as a Whole-of-Institution Approach to Curriculum and Pedagogy." *Higher Education Research and Development* 36 (4): 688–701.

Heilker, Paul, and Remi Yergeau. 2011. "Autism and Rhetoric." *College English* 73 (5): 485–97.

Hult, Christine, and the Portland Resolution Committee (David Joliffe, Kathleen Kelly, Dana Mead, and Charles Schuster). 1992. "The Portland Resolution." *WPA: Writing Program Administration* 16 (1–2): 88–94.

Isaacs, Emily, and Melinda Knight. 2014. "A Bird's Eye View of Writing Centers: Institutional Infrastructure, Scope and Programmatic Issues, Reported Practices." *WPA: Writing Program Administration* 37 (2): 36–67.

Jen, Kyle I. 2013. "State Appropriations, Tuition, and Public University Operating Costs." House Fiscal Agency Governing Committee. Accessed April 8, 2022. https://www .house.mi.gov/hfa/PDF/HigherEducation/State_Appropriations_Tuition,and_Public _University_OperatingCosts.pdf.

Johnson, Mark. "MSU Enrollment Decline Continues; Officials Hope More In-Person Classes, Campus Activities Reverse Trend." *Lansing State Journal,* March 10, 2021. https://www.lansingstatejournal.com/story/news/2021/03/10/msu-michigan-state -enrollment-decline/4636278001/.

Jones, Robert, and Joseph J. Comprone. 1993. "Where Do We Go Next in Writing Across the Curriculum?" *College Composition and Communication* 44 (1): 59–68.

Kahn, Seth. 2017. "Bad Ideas about Writing: Anybody Can Teach It." *Inside Higher Ed,* August 7, 2017. Accessed April 8, 2022. https://www.insidehighered.com/views/2017 /08/07/colleges-should-hire-writing-instructors-right-experience-and-expertise-and -give.

Kezar, Adrianna. 2006. "Redesigning for Collaboration in Learning Initiatives: An Examination of Four Highly Collaborative Campuses." *Journal of Higher Education* 77 (5): 804–38.

Kimyama, Judy Marquez, Jenny L. Lee, and Gary Rhoades. 2012. "A Critical Agency Network Model for Building an Integrated Outreach Program." *Journal of Higher Education* 83 (2): 276–303.

Kolowich, Steven. 2010. "Blasting Academic Silos." *Inside Higher Ed,* January 18, 2010. Accessed 5 April 2022. https://www.insidehighered.com/news/2010/01/18/blasting -academic-silos.

Lee, Virginia S. "Program Types and Prototypes." 2010. In Gillespie and Robertson, 21–34.

Lieberman, Devorah. 2012. "Nurturing Institutional Change: Collaboration and Leadership between Upper Level Administrators and Faculty Developers." In *Coming In from the Margins: Faculty Development's Emerging Organizational Development Role in Institutional Change,* edited by Connie Schroeder et al., 60–73. Loudoun, VA: Stylus Publishing.

Lind, Michael. 2006. "Why the Liberal Arts Still Matter." *The Wilson Quarterly* 30 (4): 52–58.

Linn, Mott. 2007. "Budget Systems Used in Allocating Resources to Libraries." *The Bottom Line: Managing Library Finance* 20 (1): 20–29.

Lockett, Alexandria, Shawanda Stewart, and Brian J. Stone. 2019. "Reflective Moments: Showcasing University Writing Program Models for Black Student Success." In Perryman-Clark and Craig, 114–40.

Maimon, Elaine P. 2000. "Preface." In McLeod and Soven, vi–xi.

Mandernach, B. Jean, Hank Radda, Scott Greenberger, and Krista Forrest. 2014. "Challenging the Status Quo: The Influence of Proprietary Learning Institutions on the Shifting Landscape of Higher Education." In *Transformative Perspectives and Processes in Higher Education*, edited by Amber Dailey-Hebert and Kay S. Dennis, 31–48. New York: Springer International.

Martini, Rebecca Hallman, and Travis Webster. 2021. "Anti-Racism Across the Curriculum: Practicing an Integrated Approach to WAC and Writing Center Faculty Development." *Writing Program Administration* 44 (3): 100–106.

Massy, William F., ed. 1996. *Resource Allocation in Higher Education*. Ann Arbor: University of Michigan Press.

McLeod, Susan H., and Margot Soven. 1989. "Writing Across the Curriculum: 1989. The Second Stage, and Beyond." *College Composition and Communication* 40 (3): 337–43.

McLeod, Susan H., and Margot Soven, eds. 2000. *Writing Across the Curriculum: A Guide to Developing Programs*. Fort Collins: WAC Clearinghouse / Colorado State University Press.

McNair, Lucy R., and Leigh Garrison-Fletcher. 2022. "Putting Languages at the Centre: Developing the Language Across the Curriculum (LAC) Faculty Seminar at LaGuardia Community College, Queens, New York." *Language, Culture and Curriculum*, no. 222, 1–15.

National Center for Education Statistics (NCES). 2016. *Projections of Education Statistics to 2016*, 35th ed. Washington, DC: US Department of Education. https://nces.ed.gov/pubs 2008/2008060_1.pdf.

National Survey of Student Engagement (NSSE). 2018. *Engagement Insights: Survey Findings on the Quality of Undergraduate Education*. https://scholarworks.iu.edu/dspace /bitstream/handle/2022/23391/NSSE_2018_Annual_Results.pdf?sequence=1&isAllo wed=y.

Nielsen, Kathryn. 2014. "Chapter 5. On Class, Race, and Dynamics of Privilege: Supporting Generation 1.5 Writers Across the Curriculum." In Zawacki and Cox, 129–50, Fort Collins: WAC Clearinghouse / Parlor Press / Colorado State University Press.

Ore, Ersula J. 2019. *Lynching: Violence, Rhetoric and American Identity*. Oxford, MS: University of Mississippi Press.

Ouellett, Mathew L. 2004. "Faculty Development and Universal Instructional Design, Equity and Excellence in Education." *Excellence in Education* 37 (32): 135–44.

Ouellett, Mathew L. 2010a. "Chapter 1: Overview of Faculty Development." In Gillespie and Robertson, 3–20.

Ouellett, Mathew L. 2010b. "Chapter 12: Overview of Diversity Issues Relating to Faculty Development." In Gillespie and Robertson, 185–202.

Perryman-Clark, Staci M. 2013. *Afrocentric Teacher-Research: Rethinking Appropriateness and Inclusion*. New York: Peter Lang.

Perryman-Clark, Staci M. 2015. "Languages, Dialects and the Myth of Edited American English." *Teachers, Profs, Parents: Writers Who Care*, no. 20. https://writerswhocare.wordpress .com/2015/10/26/languages-dialects-and-the-myth-of-edited-american-english/.

Perryman-Clark, Staci M. 2016. "Who We Are(n't) Assessing: Racializing Writing Assessment in Writing Program Administration." *College English* 17 (6): 206–11.

Perryman-Clark, Staci M. 2019. "Race, Teaching Assistants, and Student Bullying: Confessions from an African American Pre-tenured WPA." In *Defining, Locating, and Addressing Bullying in the WPA Workplace*, edited by Crystyn Elder and Beth Davila, 124–37. Logan: Utah State University Press.

Perryman-Clark, Staci M., and Collin Lamont Craig, eds. 2019. *Black Perspectives on Writing Program Administration: From the Margins to the Center.* Urbana, IL: National Council of Teachers of English (NCTE) / Conference on College Composition and Communication (CCCC) Studies in Writing and Rhetoric Series.

Perryman-Clark, Staci, David E. Kirkland, and Austin Jackson, eds. 2014. *Students' Right to Their Own Language: A Critical Sourcebook.* Boston, MA: Bedford/St. Martin's; Urbana, IL: NCTE.

Perryman-Clark, Staci, Mariam Konaté, and Jennifer Richardson. 2022. "A Time to Dream: Black Women's Exodus from White Feminist Spaces." In "Diversity Is Not an End Game: BIPOC Futures in the Academy," special issue, *Present Tense: Journal of Rhetoric in Society* 9 (2). https://www.presenttensejournal.org/volume-9/a-time-to-dream-black -womens-exodus-from-white-feminist-spaces/.

Plank, Kathryn M., and Alan Kalish. 2010. "Program Assessment for Faculty Development." In Gillespie and Robertson, 135–50.

Pod Network. n.d. "Strategic Plan and Mission." Accessed 2 Nov. 2017. https://podnetwork .org/about-us/mission/.

Porter, James E., Patricia Sullivan, Stuart Blythe, Jeffrey T. Grabill, and Libby Miles. 2000. "Institutional Critique: A Rhetorical Methodology for Change." *College Composition and Communication* 51 (4):610–42.

Powell, Malea, Daisy Levy, Andrea Riley-Mukavetz, Marilee Brooks-Gillies, Maria Novotny, and Jennifer Fisch-Ferguson. 2014. "Our Story Begins Here: Constellating Cultural Rhetorics." *Enculturation*, no. 18. Accessed 8 Nov. 2017. http://www.enculturation.net /our-story-begins-here.

Powell, Pegeen Reichert. 2009. "Retention and Writing Instruction: Implications for Access and Pedagogy." *College Composition and Communication* 60 (4): 664–82.

Price, Margaret. 2011. *Mad at School: Rhetorics of Mental Disability and Academic Life.* Ann Arbor: University of Michigan Press.

"Racial Justice Advisory Committee." Western Michigan University, September 27, 2021. https://wmich.edu/racialjusticeadvisory.

Robinson, Samuel. "WMU Track and Field Coach Kelly Lycan Fired among Accusations of Racial Insensitivity." *Western Herald,* November 4, 2019. https://www.westernherald .com/sports/article_0848c2ea-3bc2-11e9-83b6-5b9076527601.html.

Rousculp, Tiffany. 2021. "Everyone Writes: Expanding Writing Across the Curriculum to Change a Culture of Writing." In *Transformations: Change Work across Writing Programs, Pedagogies, and Practices,* edited by Holly Hassel and Kristi Cole, 105–22. Logan: Utah State University Press.

Russell, David. 1997. "Rethinking Genre and School and Society: An Activity Theory Analysis." *Written Communication* 14 (4): 504–54.

Russell, David. 1987. "Writing Across the Curriculum: Lessons from the Past." *College Composition and Communication* 38 (2): 184–94.

Rutz, Carol, William Condon, Ellen R. Iverson, Cathryn A. Manduca, and Gudrun Willett. 2012. "Faculty Professional Development and Student Learning: What Is the Relationship?" *Change: The Magazine of Higher Learning* 44 (3): 40–47.

Sandler, Karen Wiley. 2000. "Starting a WAC Program: Strategies for Administrators." In McLeod and Soven, 35–42.

Sorcinelli, Mary Deane, Ann E. Austin, and Pamela L. Eddy. 2006. *Creating the Future of Faculty Development: Learning from the Past, Understanding the Present.* Boston, MA: Anker Publishing Co.

Sullivan, Amy M., Matthew D. Lakoma, J. Andrew Billings, Antoinette S. Peters, and Susan D. Block. 2016. "Creating Enduring Change: Demonstrating the Long-Term Impact of a Faculty Development Program in Palliative Care." *Journal of General Internal Medicine* 21 (9): 907–14.

Thaiss, Christopher. 2000. "WAC and General Education Courses." In McLeod and Soven, 63–77.

"Update: Campus Climate Survey Results and RJAC Progress." Western Michigan University, May 27, 2021. wmich.edu/president/campus-climate-rjac-update.

Villanueva, Victor, and Kristin L. Arola. 2003. *Cross-Talk in Composition Theory*. Urbana, IL: National Council of Teachers of English.

Wade, Wyn Craig. 1998. *The Fiery Cross: The Ku Klux Klan in America*. New York: Oxford University Press.

Walvoord, Barbara E. 1996. "The Future of WAC." *College English* 58 (1): 58–79.

Wehlburg, Catherine M. 2010. "Assessment Practices Related to Student Learning: Transformative Assessment." In Gillespie and Robertson, 169–84.

Western Michigan University. 2019. "Institutional Research." https://wmich.edu/institutionalresearch/reportsanddashboards/enrollment.

Western Michigan University Office of Faculty Development (WMOFD). 2015. "Needs Assessment Report 2015." PDF file.

Western Michigan Office of Faculty Development (WMOFD). 2018a. "Seminar for Teaching Inclusivity Final Evaluations 2018." 2018. PDF File.

Western Michigan University. 2021a. WMU Essential Studies Data Edited.

Western Michigan University (WMU). 2021b. "WMU Foundation Receives Historic Gift in Excess of a Half-Billion Dollars, the Largest Ever for a Public Higher Ed Institution." Western Michigan University, July 8, 2021. wmich.edu/news/2021/06/64413.

Western Michigan University Strategic Plan. 2015. *The Gold Standard 2020*. https://wmich.edu/sites/default/files/attachments/u656/2016/The%20Gold%20Standard%20 2020.pdf.

Western Michigan University Strategic Resource Management (WMUSRM). 2018. "Guiding Principles." https://wmich.edu/budgetmodel/principles.

"What Is Wmux?" Western Michigan University, 14 May 2021. https://wmich.edu/x/about.

Whitford, Emma. 2021. "College Enrollments Continue to Drop This Fall." Accessed April 5, 2022. https://www.insidehighered.com/news/2021/10/26/college-enrollments-continue-drop-fall.

Wible, Scott. 2019. "Forfeiting Privilege for the Cause of Social Justice: Listening to Black WPAs and WPAs of Color Define the Work of White Allyship." In Perryman-Clark and Craig, 74–100.

Willett, Gudrun, Ellen R. Iverson, Carol Rutz, and Cathryn A. Manduca. 2014. "Measures Matter: Evidence of Faculty Development Effects on Faculty and Student Learning." *Assessing Writing*, no. 20, 19–36.

"Wmich.edu." General Education Self-Study February 15, 2016. Accessed April 5, 2022. https://wmich.edu/sites/default/files/attachments/u327/2016/MAR.pdf.

WMU Faculty Senate. 2016. "Official Memorandum of Action—MOA-16/06 General Education Revision." https://wmich.edu/sites/default/files/attachments/u370/2017/moa1606-general-education-revision-final.pdf.

WMU Faculty Senate. 2018a. "WMU Essential Studies Outcomes Rubrics." https://wmich.edu/facultysenate/wmuessentialstudies/wesrubrics.

WMU Faculty Senate. 2018b. "WMU Essential Studies Interactive Tutorials." https://wmich.edu/facultysenate/wmuessentialstudies-interactivemodel.

Worthington, Roger, Christine A. Stanley, and Daryl G. Smith. 2020. "Standards of Professional Practice for Chief Diversity Officers in Higher Education 2.0." https://nadohe.memberclicks.net/assets/2020SPPI/__NADOHE%20SPP2.0_200131_FinalFormatted.pdf.

Yergeau, Remi. 2013. "Clinically Significant Disturbance: On Theorists Who Theorize Theory of Mind." *Disability Studies Quarterly* 33 (4): n.p.

Zakrajsek, Todd D. 2010. "Chapter 6: Important Skills and Knowledge." In Gillespie. and Robertson, 83–98.

Zawacki, Terry Myers, and Michelle Cox, eds. 2014. *WAC and Second Language Writers: Research towards Linguistically and Culturally Inclusive Programs and Practices.* Columbia, SC: Parlor Press.

Zemliansky, Pavel, and Landon Berry. 2017. "A Writing-Across-the-Curriculum Faculty Development Program: An Experience Report." *IEEE Transactions on Professional Communication* 60 (3): 306–16.

Zierdt, Ginger LuAnne. 2009. "Responsibility-Centered Budgeting: An Emerging Trend in Higher Education Budget Reform." *Journal of Higher Education Policy and Management* 31 (4): 345–53.

INDEX

Locators followed by *f* indicate figures, and followed by *t* indicate tables.

ABOUT THE AUTHOR

Staci M. Perryman-Clark serves as the Director of the Institute for Intercultural and Anthropological Studies at Western Michigan University, housed within the College of Arts and Sciences. She is also professor of English and African American Studies at Western Michigan University. Perryman-Clark currently serves as the 2023 Chair of the Conference on College Composition and Communication. She is a previous recipient of the 2008 CCCC Scholars from the Dream Award; WMU College of Arts and Sciences Faculty Achievement Award in Research, Scholarship and Creative Activities; WMU College of Arts and Sciences Faculty Achievement Award in Diversity and Inclusion; and the 2020 Council of Writing Program Administrators Best Book Award.